# DRIꟻT

"In a *dérive*, one or more persons during a certain period drop their relations, their work and leisure activities, and all their other usual motives for movement and action, and let themselves be drawn by the attractions of the terrain and the encounters they find there."
— Guy Debord, *Theory of the Dérive*, 1958.

The translation of *dérive* is *drift*.

# LOS ANGELES

ADAM GOLDBERG
Editor in Chief

DANIELA VELASCO
Creative Director

ELYSSA GOLDBERG
Editorial Director

BONJWING LEE
Executive Editor


CONTRIBUTORS
Austin Langlois
Brian Gaffney
Chérmelle D. Edwards
Dale Arden Chong
Daniel Lee
David Maziarz
Duncan Nielsen
Eve Hill-Agnus
Faye Bradley
Grace Park
Imogen Lepere
Jean Trinh
Jonathan Shipley
Julie Wolfson
Lucas Oliver Oswald
Maria Belen Iturralde
Nina Gorbenko
Pete Milne
Sabrina Sucato

# DEAR READER,

More than 20 years ago, life circumstances moved me to Los Angeles. While that might be the dream for a lot of twentysomethings fresh out of college, it wasn't mine. I hated it. In fact, for the two years I lived there, and for many years thereafter, I made sure to tell every sunny face I met just how much I hated it. When I was finally able to leave, I fled to the opposite coast, eager to let Los Angeles fade far away in my rearview mirror.

So, I would seem an unlikely candidate to be introducing Drift, Volume 11, in which, this time, we issue our globetrotting postcards about coffeeland from the City of Angels.

Yet, Adam Goldberg, the publisher of these pages, asked me to pen this foreword partly because I was the only one among our small team of editors who had a personal history with the city. But perhaps more importantly—and surprisingly—I was the one who advocated most strongly in favor of making Los Angeles our next destination.

What has long been a patchwork of disparate neighborhoods, stitched together by freeways, boulevards, beaches, and canals, the greater Los Angeles area has, in the past decade, experienced an exciting renaissance of culture. Once a city dominated by old diners and taco stands, Hollywood haunts and chain restaurants, this sprawling metropolis by the sea is now also home to a rapidly diversifying independent restaurant and coffee scene.

But beside this glittering growth is struggle and hardship. The COVID pandemic and growing racial and social justice awareness have highlighted tears in the fabric of our American society. For many of us, the last 18 months have been difficult. And in this issue, we spotlight Los Angeles to showcase those who are mending America's unique and colorful quilt with their work in the coffee industry.

From the industrial port of Long Beach to the dry, hot hills above Malibu, our contributors bring you stories of ambition and empathy, setbacks and triumphs. Julie Wolfson takes us to a new Chinatown, where a rising generation of Asian Americans are reestablishing a footing in a forgotten corner. Pete Milne visits the beach volleyball courts in the sandy South Bay, where Brian Gaffney finds Colombian specialty coffee. In Filipinotown, Jean Trinh talks with the Harris brothers, who are reimagining community in their coffee shop from a Black perspective. And everywhere, Imogen Lepere notices coffee shop owners are welcoming furry, four-legged friends to their outdoor patios.

Los Angeles isn't only the capital of America's shiniest export—pop culture—it is home to a vibrant community of people that has given me a new perspective and appreciation for a city I once left behind. Whether you're a native Angeleno, transplant, visitor, or a reader in parts unknown, I hope you discover, as I did, something wonderful and new about this dynamic city.

*BONJWING LEE,*
*EXECUTIVE EDITOR*

# Riding the Hallyu

WORDS
Dale Arden Chong

PHOTOGRAPHS
Adam Goldberg, Daniela Velasco

It's 2021, and the world is undoubtedly caught in *hallyu*, otherwise known as the Korean Wave. Chinese journalists first coined the term—which, in Chinese, translates to "Korean wave"—in the 1990s to describe the spike in the popularity of South Korean entertainment around the world, marking the country's influence on global culture. The phenomenon of Korean pop culture taking over the global market, with its ever-popular beauty products, television dramas, and, of course, pop music, couldn't be summed up in a better way than this simple word. If you pause to think about it, *hallyu* might seem less like a tidal wave and more like a tsunami. We see this with bands like BTS and award-winning films like Bong Joon-ho's "Parasite," drawing eyes from all around the world towards South Korea and everything it produces. However, another aspect of Korean culture may be at the heart of it all: *jeong*.

"In the general sense, *jeong* is the personal connection and relationship that you cultivate through time, but also in that space, together," Joonmo Kim, the co-founder of MARU, a coffee shop in the Arts District and Los Feliz neighborhoods of Los Angeles, shared. "I think it comes from a very collective culture and society in Asia, but especially in Korea." According to MARU's other founder, Jacob Park, you can think of *jeong* as an unbreakable bond. "Even if someone does a bad thing to me, I still give him my love and won't expect anything in return." Both Kim and Park cite examples of *jeong* between two individuals, but they also explain how *jeong* permeates through a community, too—more specifically, their coffee shops.

One of the first things Kim and Park will share is that MARU represents more than two people. The founders emphasize that the MARU experience starts with its staff, which is considered family. However, it also involves the relationships created between their staff and customers, as well as among customers themselves. "At first, there were four of us: us and two baristas. That's been the core of the company, so I think it started from there. After that, our customers made it better," Park explained. "Our customers will sit next to each other without knowing each other, but then they start talking and become friends. It's not just our team; our customers make the community strong." Park, who grew up in South Korea, shared that these organic relationships among those in MARU's orbit feel unexpected. Of course, it doesn't hurt that everyone who goes to the neighborhood spots embraces the brand's approach to coffee.

While other coffee companies and roasters create their blends with complex flavors, MARU pares its roasts down to focus on a unique and straightforward flavor. "Jacob's the mastermind behind all the coffee. He's always looking for that unique flavor to bring to the customers," Kim said. "We try to find coffees that are single cultivar, meaning there's less complexity to it, but there's a particular taste for that coffee." He explained that their philosophy for coffee is taking what already exists and trying to do it better. This emphasis on the depth and flavor—and to leave a specific memory in the process—is why MARU's customers keep coming back.

MARU's unique approach to coffee stems from its founders' shared goal of making coffee their way: high quality with distinct flavors. That said, they also wanted to serve their community in both presentation and experience. "It comes from our Korean culture, like plating food. We were always thinking about how we can combine quality and presentation," Park said. Kim and Park, who each spent large parts of their upbringing in Korea, expressed how the importance of each factor is ubiquitous to their background. "We were always seeing our moms, aunts, and

Adrian Cervantes, Cesar Vazquez, & Beau Bray

grandmas make everything. There are so many hands that go into creating a dish, both in the way it's prepared and how it's presented. There's a lot of effort and heart that goes into it, so we wanted to emulate that same experience for our customers," Kim shared. It's this sense of community and togetherness, which stems from building *jeong* with one another, that has led MARU's founders to put a lot of thought into every part of their brand.

One example of how MARU executes this idea is how they choose to serve their customers. Kim explains that on a perfect day, a customer could order a macchiato and have it fully prepared and plated on a wooden tray with a napkin, a spoon, and a sparkling tea as a palate cleanser before one of the staff members would bring it to the table. "There's a lot of respect within our culture, whether it's towards the process, the food, or the product. We want to carry through our brand," Kim explained.

Park drew inspiration for the peaceful MARU experience from a Buddhist temple in the mountains—where he spent his childhood. "L.A. is very trendy, and it changes really fast. It's a tough market," Park observed. "The city's ever-changing coffee scene made me want to go back to my roots, more classic and original." Both he and Kim wanted to keep MARU true to who they are; it was only a coincidence that they launched during the height of the Korean Wave and, in the best way, were caught in the current.

MARU's founders said that they launched at the right time when the world began to dive further into Korean culture. "Every time I see K-pop in the mainstream media, it blows my mind. Like, it *really* blows my mind," Kim shared as he discussed the growing attention on Korean culture in the United States. "I used to listen to Korean music in high school while driving my car, and every time another car pulled up next to me, I would turn it down because people would make fun of it. I think we've progressed a lot culturally with more diversity, but really, I think it's just such a great time to be Asian."

It's likely Los Angeles feels this sentiment more strongly than other cities—L.A. County is home to the largest Korean population in the country. At the same time, the city itself is a cultural hub for the latest entertainment and pop culture trends. And though some of the most significant Korean movements to grab the world's attention are inherently rooted in the city, parts of its Korean culture still return to the tradition of simplicity, which brings us back to *jeong*.

*Jeong* is both collective and personal—and at the end of the day, it's built through raw, human connection. Of course, creating these deep and meaningful relationships can also lead to vulnerability—something Kim noted as he described the concept. But it also leads to a community-focused level of care. "*Jeong* definitely has a strong correlation with family. You're close, but you have to care for one another, so no one gets hurt," he said. "However, I'd rather have *jeong* whether you get hurt or not, because that's what humans are all about: having this type of relationship and heart for one another." In an era when everyone is relearning how to be with one another again, *jeong* might be the most important thing we have.

—

# Sipping and Strolling in New Chinatown

WORDS
Julie Wolfson

PHOTOGRAPHS
Daniela Velasco

In downtown Los Angeles's historic Chinatown, the Thien Hau temple, the colorful sites of Central Plaza, and the romantic allure of the galleries along Chung King Road create a visual feast for the eyes. From classic restaurants and new food stalls to traditional bakeries and modern tea shops, the neighborhood cooks up sensory adventures. New Chinatown was built in the 1930s after the Chinese community was relocated from the original location that is now Union Station. The new area was built with grit and tenacity and hard work by the original founding families, many of which still own buildings in the neighborhood today. Peking ducks hang in steamy windows. The scent of strawberry cream cakes wafts out of Phoenix Bakery. The sights and sounds of parades and festivals fill the air. And to top it all off, Chinatown is home to some of the city's best coffee bars.

Inside Far East Plaza, Jack Benchakul has been serving coffee in one of L.A.'s most revered coffee shops since 2015. Born in N.Y.C. but raised in L.A., Benchakul has been visiting L.A.'s Chinatown since he was 7 years old. His journey from a career in science to opening Endorffeine offers some clues into why drinking coffee with Benchakul has become a notable Los Angeles cafe experience. Benchakul, a former biochemist, worked in biotech for over 11 years at some of the biggest companies developing cancer-fighting drugs. He found himself thinking about food and drink and attended culinary school in the evenings and weekends. He apprenticed at Michelin star restaurants and patisseries. Then, at the Blue Bottle cart at the San Francisco Ferry Building, Benchakul had a cup of coffee that blew his mind, served to him by Blue Bottle's founder James Freeman.

This cup made Benchakul think more about specialty coffee. He started reading and brewing at home. When he moved back to L.A. to work at a biopharmaceutical company, he kept thinking about coffee. A job search led him to take a job at Cafe Demitasse in Little Tokyo, when they first opened in 2011. Next up was a stint at Yeekai Lim's Cognoscenti Coffee in Culver City. Lim, an architect, had changed his focus from designing buildings to creating an ideal coffee shop. Benchakul and Lim, both exploring their new career paths, bonded over their desire to craft high-quality espresso and brewed coffee drinks.

Then Benchakul felt ready to branch out on his own. He envisioned a coffee cart and eventually a cafe where he could tinker with the science of coffee until he could reach his desired level of perfection. Benchakul built the cart and popped up inside the modern Vietnamese cafe Good Girl Dinette in Highland Park. That's when Benchakul met George Yu, who suggested he check out Far East Plaza in Chinatown

"You can't tell what is going on at Far East Plaza from the street side," says Benchakul. Yu suggested he try popping up inside of Scoops Ice Cream. Chris Gere of Chinatown Scoops immediately agreed to the idea. Benchakul rolled his cart into Scoops, where he served coffee inside the shop for a year. The opportunity gave him the chance to try out the neighborhood and reinforce his instinct that Chinatown was the right place for his first shop, Endorffeine. "It felt like there was a lot of energy that was building under the surface. For a budding entrepreneur, you want to be on the ground floor. It's always great to grow within a community too. It's cool to be a part of that beginning," he says. "That's when we started building out the space next door to Scoops."

In the last decade Far East Plaza has been home to Cantonese food, Thai noodles, Japanese breakfast pop-ups, Taiwanese street food, Scoops Ice Cream, Lasita Filipino rotisserie chicken, Roy

Jack Benchakul, Endorffeine

Jack Benchakul, Endorffeine

Choi's Chego, Alvin Cailan's Amboy, and the ever-lengthening lines of Howlin Ray's Nashville hot chicken. "Far East Plaza is a food centric scene," explains Benchakul. "Roy Choi described it as a hawker center. For me, it reminds me of food centers in Bangkok with the influence of different backgrounds." The culinary community gathers at night for Chinatown After Dark and other special events, where Jessica Wang has served her Pique-Nique desserts and Royce Burke his Secret Lasagna.

In the midst of these vibrant flavors, Endorffeine is a serene haven. Benchakul along with his cousin Ttaya Tuparungsi designed their minimalist space. "When Ttaya and I started to think about where to open up a space. We wanted something in the heart of the action," says Benchakul. "There is a lot of hustle and bustle in downtown L.A. There is an energy there that is like Tokyo or Bangkok."

Endorffeine features dual Modbar drip heads for pulling shots of espresso and a setup for individual pour overs. Each corner of the counter is anchored by a grinder, a Mahlkonig EK 43 for coffee, and a Mazzer for espresso. Tuparungsi greets customers and, since day one, Benchakul has made every cup of coffee. "I learn every single time I make a brew." To this day they have never hired an additional barista.

"Most people don't know that every week, since the very beginning, I have batched our water recipe. I strip out everything and add back in calcium, magnesium, bicarbonate, and other things that will help extract certain aromatics and flavors in the coffee." Benchakul prefers Nordic style roasts and carries a rotating roster of beans roasted by Sey, Drop, Prolog, and Coffee Collective to serve and sell. "These lighter roasts complement my water chemistry. When done well you get a lot of fruit forwardness in a Nordic roast. It finishes clean, sometimes with a lingering sweetness," says Benchakul.

"We wanted to strip away everything that is superfluous. What remained is Endorffeine." By day Endorffeine serves coffee and a series of batched cold brew and tea drinks. Food is only served on nights when Endorffeine offers a seated, tasting menu of desserts made by Benchakul paired with coffee and tea. He's soon launching a line of canned beverages. The first series will feature: Butterfly flower tea, matcha coconut tea, Thai iced coffee, and vanilla-pandan coffee.

"A barista is really like the conductor of an orchestra," he says. "All of the pieces, the instruments are there. It's a matter of what we bring forward and what we hold back and how we connect that first sip and first perceptions of flavor to the lingering [after-notes]. It's all about balance. That's how we are approaching the future of Chinatown too," he adds. "How do we continue to complement the community? How do we continue to do our part and keep the balance? Now as everything changes, more people are trying to do good and exist as a community."

Leaving Far East Plaza and heading up Broadway, with a cup of coffee from Endorffeine in hand, visitors can stroll by the colorful Central Plaza buildings and pay a visit to the Bruce Lee statue. On Hill Street, Chinatown Central Plaza building has become home to new cafes and shops and a colorful patio designed by Julie and Jeff Lien, the designers and owners of the Chunky Paper gift shop (now open in the historic Hop Louie building). Inside, until recently, Vivian Ku of Pine & Crane and Joy served Taiwanese breakfast dishes at Today Starts Here. Sesame L.A. is a neighborhood superette filled with culinary

Jack Benchakul, Endorffeine

pantry items, local produce, and fresh flowers. And you'll find Thank You Coffee operating in symbiosis with Paper Please, a small stationery shop.

Jonathan Yang of Thank You Coffee, who originally started his coffee career at a cafe on the campus of UCSD, has also worked at Bird Rock, LAMILL, and Café Dulce. He founded Thank You Coffee with Matt Chung and Cody Wang. In early 2020, Friedia Niimura and Christine Kim opened their contemporary stationary shop Paper Please in Chinatown. They began to look for a coffee company that would want to set up inside their store and reached out to Yang on Instagram. He immediately drove up to Chinatown with a La Marzocco mini, plugged it in and made them two cappuccinos. What began as a pop-up became a partnership and the two companies moved to the Hill Street location together.

Currently, Thank You Coffee is serving drinks made with beans roasted by B&W, Colonna, Calendar, Manhattan, and House Roots Coffee. When asked why he was so enthusiastic about the location, Yang recalls childhood memories of Chinatown. "This is where we stayed with our grandma and she took us walking around when we were kids," says Yang. "My mom was born in Indonesia and moved to Shanghai with my grandma. Then my grandma moved to Hong Kong before coming to the U.S. in the 1960s, straight to Chinatown. I grew up in Temple City."

"Serving coffee in Chinatown has helped me better understand Chinatown. I saw the sign that says New Chinatown and wanted to know why it is not called Old Chinatown and I found an article that explained how New Chinatown came to be. Central Plaza was the first plaza in New Chinatown. These founding families, against all odds, were able to purchase and develop this piece of land," says Yang. "For me Chinatown is a place that is essential to the history of Chinese Americans. It took so much work to establish and is so significant—and there would have been no opportunity to move eastward to San Gabriel Valley (where there is a significant Chinese-American population) without Chinatown."

"Now being in the Hill Street building, we wanted to stay in Chinatown. There is something magical about stationery and coffee and the culture that it creates. We both want to support each other." says Yang. Yang's wife Julia has taken on the role of graphic design and art director. Being in a stationery store influences their branding and growing sticker collection.

For the menu, Yang draws on the flavors that complement Chinese culture. "Being in Chinatown made me comfortable and confident reaching into the flavors I grew up with," he says. "The first drink introduced was the "You're Welcome Latte" made with *lapsang souchong* (a smoked Chinese black tea), chicory pecan bitters, sugar, espresso, and oat milk. We make a simple syrup with the tea and the bitters. It is inspired by Chinese barbecue with the smoke and the wood."

The Thank You Coffee menu also features a *hojicha* latte. "We grew up drinking milk tea. It is a big part of Cantonese culture," says Yang. "When Julia Yang came back from a trip to Kyoto, she brought some *hojicha* from a street market that we both loved." Now Yang pan-roasts his own to get as close to that flavor as possible. He also created a Five Spice Latte with a custom 10-spice blend adding chili flakes, MSG, cardamom, and ginger to complement espresso and milk. "Growing up in San Gabriel Valley—we love big flavors," he adds.

With the vibrant new culinary and retail offerings on Hill Street, the intentions of each company are clear. They talk about their desire to honor the neighborhood and respect the culture and the community. With the serenity and scientific precision at Endorffeine and the creative latte recipes with Chinese ingredients at Thank You Coffee, both coffee experiences do just that.

—

# COVID Coffee, No Sugar:
# Old L.A. Diners' Pandemic Struggles

WORDS
Jonathan Shipley

ILLUSTRATION
Grace Park

"Everything was so terrible. The psychological damage; the brutality of it," reflects Paul Rosenbluh, co-owner of one of the oldest diners in Los Angeles, on the havoc COVID wreaked on his restaurant, Cindy's Eagle Rock outside Pasadena. Rosenbluh co-owns the restaurant with his wife, Monique King. They're both chefs, and during the hardest months of the pandemic, Rosenbluh asked himself again and again, "What the hell are we going to do?" They couldn't sell their buttermilk pancakes, nor their shrimp and grits. They couldn't serve their fried chicken and eggs. Coffee mugs sat lined up, pristine and unused as the pandemic shut it all down. "I can usually find a silver lining," he says, "but I can't for this. There hasn't been one for this."

This pandemic, however, might be easing up enough for Rosenbluh to see some light. Vaccines are now widely available. At the time of writing, Los Angeles County is reporting decreases in both COVID cases and hospitalizations. The restaurant industry is ready to take a brief sigh of relief, through a mask. "I just want to get back to business as usual," Rosenbluh says. "Just some semblance of what we had before."

This is a common refrain in the industry, particularly with the coffee shops and old-school diners in Los Angeles County that have been in business the longest. Some of these places have become celebrated institutions and the storm of COVID has shaken their very foundations.

"I always wanted to own a diner," Rosenbluh says. Cindy's Eagle Rock is the third restaurant collaboration with his wife. They opened and operated the fine dining establishment Firefly Bistro in South Pasadena for 12 years. When Cindy's Eagle Rock was up for sale, they were asked if they were interested in buying it. "We loved the idea of it." Work commenced. "It's been here since

1948 but it's older than that. It was absolutely a greasy spoon."
From the commencement of work, it looks like no work had been
done to the restaurant at all. The walk-in cooler was made of
wood and insulated with sawdust. The pie case was one of a kind.
The place "existed," he says. "That's about all I can say about the
place—it existed."

They renovated it, updated the menu (everything is now made
from scratch, including the popular chorizo sausage), and
started offering high-end coffee. "We serve coffee from local
Jones Coffee Roasters. It's just a great cup of coffee," he says.
"Family-owned, [Jones Coffee Roasters] gets their beans from
their own plantation in Guatemala." With good food and good
vibes, people came to Cindy's again and again. The regularity
of customers, as opposed to their high-end establishment, was
something Rosenbluh and King especially liked about the diner.
"You get to build relationships with people." A young man comes
in one day for breakfast. A couple months later he might come
in with his girlfriend. A year later, they're eating as husband and
wife. A year or two later, they're bringing their kids. "You see
slices of their lives and they see ours," Rosenbluh enthuses.

People came to the diner, until they couldn't. The pandemic shut
it all down for a hard stretch of time. "We had to pivot and pivot
and pivot. It's been really hard."

It hasn't just been hard on Cindy's Eagle Rock, it has been
hard everywhere. Saugus Cafe, originally named the Tolfree
Saugus Eating House, first opened in 1888, the same year as
the Washington Monument. It is the oldest restaurant in Los
Angeles County. Hollywood greats like John Wayne and Charlie
Chaplin have eaten there. Teddy Roosevelt once bellied up to a
steak there and called it "splendid." Yecenia Mercado, the current
owner, inherited the business from her father. "I refuse to see all
of my dad's hard work go down the drain," she said during the
pandemic. She set up a Go Fund Me campaign to keep things
afloat. For a time, ownership didn't think it would last another
week without help. Luckily, restrictions eased, allowing open-air
dining in addition to take-out orders, and vaccines were rolled
out. The oldest restaurant is now older still. A Yelp reviewer
recently visited. "[Yecenia] made sure we were taken care of and
kept our coffee cups full."

Since 1924, the Original Pantry Cafe has been full of customers. It's owned by former Los Angeles Mayor Richard Riordan. The diner touts itself as being open 24 hours a day, every day of the year. They've been dishing up classic American fare for decades and pouring hot cups of joe for everyone from celebrities, like Marilyn Monroe and Martin Luther King, Jr., to down-on-your-luck joes who call nearby Skid Row home. "You see people of all walks of life," Rosenbluh says of a diner.

Keeping the Original Pantry Cafe open was a struggle in a year when their pre-pandemic annual average of serving 10.5 tons of coffee dwindled to a trickle (they use Gavina Coffee, an importer and roaster located in Vernon, California). They had to adjust, and adjust again hoping for a "new normal" that may be coming one day soon.

But, will anything be normal again? Is there going back? For 101 Coffee Shop in Hollywood, which closed in early 2021 due to the pandemic, there is not. In a statement, co-owner Warner Ebbink said, "Because of the ongoing pandemic, the temporary closure of the 101 Coffee Shop has become permanent." The statement continued, "We'll always be grateful for the shared moments and what the restaurant brought to the L.A. food and beverage community."

"I'm mentally exhausted," Rosenbluh admits as some approximation of a COVID finish line seems within view to him and the other cafe owners. He's tired of having to reinvent the restaurant time and again as the rules and regulations of COVID dining fluctuate as much as COVID cases have spiked, fallen, and spiked again. He's tired of just trying to survive. Most of his staff is gone. Many, he notes, have left the state, and some have left the industry entirely. "I just want us to do our jobs again." That means serving a young man sitting at the counter having brisket hash. A waiter pours the young man a cup of coffee, asking about how he's fairing in the pandemic. They chat warmly. The scene is a slice of life. The cup gets refilled, steam rising.

—

# That Golden Glow

WORDS
Eve Hill-Agnus

PHOTOGRAPHS
Adam Goldberg, Daniela Velasco

It would be difficult to tell the story of L.A. without mentioning Grand Central Market. On Broadway Street downtown, the turn-of-the-century edifice was greeted with fanfare when it opened as the city's largest public market in 1917. It brought together two buildings, the Homer Laughlin (1897) and its annex (1905), to become the first steel-reinforced structure in Southern California. As a teenager, I loved its architecture: the columns that still punctuate the space inside, as well as the Million Dollar Theater next door, with gargoyles and a profusion of balustrades in the Beaux-Arts style. I loved equally the way it presented a microcosm of the mosaic of L.A.

I knew the market over the years as a collection of everything culturally that defined the city, a kaleidoscopic melting pot. It was a warren of stalls long-held by Latino vendors with names like Valeria's Chiles & Spices and La Huerta Candy & Sweets and Sarita's Pupuseria. People on their lunch breaks sat on stools for *antojitos Mexicanos*, nestled in among produce stalls mounded with dried chiles.

But there were periods when its vibrancy lapsed. Downtown endured neglect, and at times, the market's gap-toothed corridors of empty stalls reflected that.

From the job and life across the country, to which I'd reluctantly moved after college, I watched and took note periodically when I visited.

Thankfully, by the mid-aughts, new owners revitalized the grand dame, and the market became a place where skaters in full skate wear bumping up against dark *mole*, thick as fudge, created a vibrant, multi-faceted tableau. I told skeptics, who were cognizant of what downtown had been, "No, you must come. It's a mosaic. It's a city of wonders."

G&B Coffee rode this revival wave into the market, opening in 2013. It actually started as a tiny caffeination pop-up in Jessica Koslow's cult breakfast-lunch spot Sqirl in 2012. Founders Kyle Glanville and Charles Babinski (for whom G&B is named) were both alumni of the Intelligentsia coffee shop located in Silver Lake, where they had worked together. Babinski left the company in 2020, but both are U.S. Barista Champions and Glanville had already opened three Intelligentsia locations in L.A. when they went out on their own.

Later, G&B's sister business Go Get Em Tiger would become a juggernaut, with a well-sourced roasting operation and retail tendrils reaching across the city in a boomerang from Santa Monica to Highland Park to West Hollywood. But when they opened the stand-alone G&B (which was and still is the only coffee shop with that name) in Grand Central Market, GGET still only had one shop, in Larchmont Village. Both wanted downtown L.A. to be ground zero for a new California-based coffee service style. The format: walk up and order from all four sides of the marble-topped bar.

I remember my first visit to G&B Coffee. It was just after it was remodeled in 2015. It was a typical Angeleno day, with light spilling down in a golden wash from Bunker Hill, alighting on the Angels Flight funicular and flowering jacaranda that march down the hill. I was captivated by G&B's new way of doing coffee, and I admired its innovative spirit.

I kept an early copy of the menu, with a comic book-style illustration on the cover and a slightly funky sans-serif font

typeface that looked hand-lettered. An inside page introduced you to "The Magical World of One & Ones," depicting side-by-side split-shot espresso drinks like the Dark and Stormy, which included a shot of espresso, but also ginger beer and a house caramelized sugar syrup. This world of barista competition-style tricks (usually merely single shots with and without milk) approached with Willy Wonka glee was a vision of what was to come. Though technically and ideologically serious in everything it did, G&B wasn't afraid to offer a menu that felt like a whimsical children's book.

I remember that you could get an iced almond-macadamia latte, which The New York Times hailed as the best iced latte in America in 2014, or almond-macadamia milk with turmeric, fresh ginger, honey, and black pepper or a Lil Oaty, pecan-macadamia oat milk with espresso and vegan coconut caramel.

Regulars knew to order waffles clad in ricotta and jam or cornmeal-cheddar savory ones spread with butter and honey.

It was a hangout. It was a chill-spot. It was a place to stand or perch on one of 18 stools and lean in as one would at a beloved watering hole. (Its flow was in fact devised by a well-known Los Angeles bar designer.) Initially, G&B used all different roasters but eventually settled on using coffee roasted by its sister operation, Go Get Em Tiger (GGET). It did not have time-consuming pour overs. Rather, it offered batch brews for filter aficionados, and a bar lead to help choreograph service efficiently around the central island, a well-synchronized modern dance.

As G&B blossomed, the surrounding stalls would contribute to the market's zeitgeist, one where everything was buzzing and exciting.

The more than 100-year-old edifice became an incubator for culinary newcomers, who the Los Angeles Times food section and the culinary cognoscenti celebrated as *enfants terribles*. Key players like Eggslut, which brought lines with a 45-minute to two-hour wait for Alvin Cailin's bronzed brioche sandwiches cradling pillowy eggs and cheese, helped reinvigorate the Grand Central Market. Sari Sari Store breached the fray with Filipino *buko* pie thick with young coconut and dreamy custard, Filipino rice bowls of adobo-marinated pork, and fluffy *pandesal*.

I made it my religion to go there every time I went back home. Always, it felt like touching a cultural lodestone. But I will never forget that first encounter with that almond-macadamia latte that launched a thousand flurries of alternative milk-besotted coffee fans. That morning, when G&B felt like a revelation, helped me to understand my city better. It feels long ago now, when specialty coffee was new and had a magical pull, but the light was, as ever, pale and golden in L.A.

—

Bloom & Plume

# Building Community

WORDS
Jean Trinh

PHOTOGRAPHS
Daniel Lee

In early 2020, a customer at Sip & Sonder in Inglewood told the coffee shop's co-owner Shanita Nicholas that she wanted to be with her Black community to grieve the death of Kobe Bryant.

This exchange was particularly poignant for Nicholas. She realized how important her space, which she created with her partner Amanda-Jane Thomas, had become in the neighborhood. "There [are] lots of ways community shows up: a lot of programming that you get to put on, and then, times to be together," Nicholas, 34, explained.

Sip & Sonder is one of a number of Black-owned coffee shops in L.A. that have been building and challenging the notions of what it means to create spaces for Black communities.

Bloom & Plume Coffee in Historic Filipinotown is another such place. Its purple facade adds a pop of color to Temple Boulevard, with luscious greenery overhanging the entrance of the shop. Inside, beautiful flower arrangements and artwork add to the ambiance. It's owned by brothers Maurice and Moses Harris. The former is a high-end florist with celebrity clients, and the latter is a corporate banker.

Maurice Harris, 40, wanted to create a stunning space designed for people of color and non-heteronormative clients, but one that would still make everyone feel welcome. "I feel like in the spaces where I go to shop or eat, I'm not really considered in the presentation of these experiences," he says. "It was not curated for me. I just have to take what I can get. And so, I wanted to create a space where people like me—that like nice things, that like a beautiful experience—we're centered in the end."

At Bloom & Plume, there's also a nuanced experience for Black customers—a hidden coded language, Maurice Harris says. For example, their menu is printed on church fans, a nod to the fact that the Harris brothers grew up going to a Black church.

Sip & Sonder's proprietors, both lawyers who met in New York, also wanted to create a place where they felt like they belonged. Nicholas says when she left Brooklyn, where gentrification was a major issue, she didn't feel very welcomed in the borough's coffee shops.

Nicholas remembers the day she and Thomas, who has a background in sociology, came up with the idea of opening Sip & Sonder. It was something that arose from their discussions about placemaking, a philosophy and approach behind building public spaces that promote the well-being of communities. "Maybe these two areas aren't so disparate, and they can come together in a way of utilizing coffee as a conduit to placemaking and community building," Nicholas says.

Pre-pandemic, the partners would host jazz music nights and art exhibitions as ways to build access for and engage with the community. They now use their sidewalk space to host pop-ups in collaboration with small businesses.

Sip & Sonder has an in-house roaster, and the women make it a point to educate their customers about where their coffee comes from. "It's been an incredible journey to understand on an even deeper level that coffee [beans are] picked by Black and Brown hands," Nicholas says. "And we get to serve it in a Black and Brown community, and [bring] that level of connectivity, education, and empowerment, [and] share [it] with the community around us."

Maurice Morris

There's a similar connection to the source of coffee at Silverback Coffee of Rwanda in Echo Park. Rwandan founder Jack Karuletwa makes it a point to donate a percentage of his cafe's proceeds toward helping the people of Rwanda affected by genocide, by supporting organizations that build schools and help widows and orphans, as well as care for Silverback gorillas.

Hot & Cool Cafe in Leimert Park has also become a cultural hub in its community. When Anthony Jolly, a roaster who's had over 20 years of experience in the coffee industry, first came to South L.A., he wanted to address the fact that the area is a food desert. He put the coffee program on the back burner in the beginning so he could focus on bringing healthful vegan options to the neighborhood.

Jolly, 47, put a suggestion box on his front door and "gave the keys to the community," he says. He accepted any and all requests for events, and has since provided a space for musical performances, real estate and cooking classes, and after-school programs. He's in the midst of developing a program to train the youth and formerly incarcerated individuals on barista skills.

Jolly didn't originally set out to be so community-focused, as he's conservative in how he does business, but he felt compelled to do something once he landed in Leimert Park. "It's hard not to be part of a community when you're a minority … not only Blacks, but Hispanics and Asians … [You have] the same suffering, same understanding, same fears …."

Building community is a tough subject for the Harris brothers, who are struggling to keep Bloom & Plume open. As a byproduct, they don't have the time and money to invest in the community like they've wanted.

"It's a double-edged sword—who pays for community to exist? Usually, the onus is on people that can't afford it," Maurice Harris observes.

He says their business plan was flawless and they looked great on paper, but they still got rejected 40 times for a Small Business Administration (SBA) bank loan to open the cafe, and didn't qualify for a second Paycheck Protection Program (PPP) loan in the pandemic. His brother Moses, 34, notes, "SBA loans to Black-owned businesses have plummeted over the last 15 years. And the number one reason why is because Black people don't have collateral."

The brothers say they don't have the answers, but they do feel the government should step in to help minority-owned businesses stay afloat. If not, communities that are forgotten will stay forgotten.

"I want to show Black children about entrepreneurship and the stock market," Moses Harris explains. "And it's important for Black queer folks to have a place to call home…. But the other part of that story is we have to tell the whole truth. Why is this place barely hanging on? Yeah, we want it to be a community hub, but how long can we sustain it? How long can we be here? That is the ugly truth."

—

# Venice of America

WORDS
Maria Belen Iturralde

PHOTOGRAPHS
Nina Gorbenko, Pete Milne, Daniela Velasco

Venice Beach, the ever-colorful, ever-charming pocket of sunshine on the west side of Los Angeles, ceaselessly and effortlessly attracts locals and newcomers alike.

Its sunny streets, peppered with relaxed restaurants, vibrant murals, bohemian boutiques, and first-rate coffee shops lure eclectic crowds from across the city and, arguably, the globe, for the area's unique and vibrant energy. The sun-bleached boulevards are lined with slender palm trees and garnished with art, each clamoring for attention among the brightly colored bougainvilleas. The salty air carries with it a gentle quality and everything seems to be constantly draped in warm, amber-colored hues. In less residential streets, the smell of espresso floats about in the sea breeze, prompting visitors to seek respite from the California heat by stepping into one of the area's outstanding cafes. At twilight, clouds threaded with pink and gold drift slowly across candy-colored skies.

"It's America's global village—a place where the visitor becomes part of the spectrum of what is happening," said filmmaker Marc Madow. "It's all about sharing talents, skills, music, food, and art. A message in a bottle of what California is all about."

Venice is eclectic, multicultural, ebullient, relaxed, extraordinary, electric. And its coffee scene is no exception. Its coffee shops cater to a wide range of cultures. Espresso is served alongside skate, surf, and sea breeze, and any and all are welcome.

Initially a swampy marshland, Venice has become a global destination for tourists and a welcomed escape for Californians from all walks of life. And it all started with one man.

New Jersey native Abbot Kinney famously recovered from asthma after spending a night sleeping on a pool table in a Southern Californian hotel and decided, then and there, to settle in this corner of the world. He began purchasing property around the area, eventually buying a portion of the Ocean Park Casino and the land around it with his business partner and building a beach resort that went by the same name. When his partner passed away, the company was dissolved and the property divided. Kinney chose to keep the less developed area further south—a blank canvas where he could build "Venice of America" to emulate his favorite European city and spur on a social and cultural revival.

Kinney sought to create a place for intellectual pursuits and leisure. To that end, he built a complex canal network, a pier, a ship cafe, an auditorium, a yacht club, among other attractions. It opened in the summer of 1905 to 40,000 visitors, who explored the newly developed area aboard gondolas and a custom-built, miniature railroad. Kinney kept pushing for the development to be a place for higher learning and education, but visitors favored the neighborhood's amusement park persona and that is what prevailed.

Over the course of 116 years, Venice's colorful culture authored a kaleidoscope history.

It was annexed by the city of Los Angeles in 1926 and went on to become an oil drilling site in the 1930s, a bodybuilding hub in the 1950s, a home for beatniks and hippies in the 1960s, a skateboarding mecca in the 1970s (home to the world-famous "Z-Boys"), and a punk-rock center in the 1980s. Taking on multiple personalities, Venice has refused to accede to anyone else's definition of what it "should be." Its principal *raison d'être* is simple: its people. There are no rules but those of its dwellers, which is why, over a century later, Venice is still in one of its many stages of metamorphosis.

Menotti's

The character of its cafes inevitably follows this ethos.

Over the past decade or so, an appreciation for quality brews and third wave coffee has paved the way for a new type of cafe to emerge in Venice. Alongside national names like Blue Bottle and Intelligentsia came local establishments like Superba, Gjusta, Menotti's, and the revamped version of The Rose. Each of these homegrown businesses introduced a different set of rules for what a cafe should be and have adapted and grown to its unique community.

They're places where one can go for an excellent cup of coffee, or a glass of wine, or a terrific pastry, or an altogether superb meal. They're about the food, the atmosphere, the people, and—to quote the Venetian vernacular—the *vibe*.

"Venice has allowed us to play with different aspects of what this form of hospitality could look like, without a lot of narrative," says Shelley Kleyn Armistead, partner and COO of the Gjelina Group. "[Gjusta] started with three items on the menu and we've slowly grown [it] into the ginormous octopus that she is today. And I think Venice has always been incredibly kind in not asking us to have a huge amount of narrative around what we are. We've never truly identified what we are because we leave scope for openness to keep learning and figuring out when we want to move or change...and [Venice] just lets us be."

Few places capture the neighborhood's essence so superbly as does Gjusta, the Gjelina Group's famed Sunset Avenue restaurant housed discreetly behind a nondescript storefront. Initially a commissary kitchen known for its sourdough loaves with crisp, golden crusts, it has evolved into much more than a bakery.

Sitting on Gjusta's sun-dappled patio, Armistead explained how it "slowly took on a life of its own." Today, Gjusta continues to operate a bread program, but also offers pantry staples, smoked fish, rotisserie items, deli products, butchery, wine, home goods, and an array of pastries that have acquired nationwide fame.

The coffee, she says, was created to be "everyday, uncomplicated, and a little industrial, like the space itself," which speaks to the cafe's relaxed, accessible ethos. On any given day, patrons can pair a first-rate cup of coffee—served in handmade ceramic mugs—with one of the scrumptious treats in the pastry case, or enjoy any of the offerings on the extensive menu. Come afternoon, when the strings of lights hanging above the patio are on and the sky has taken on a violet-orange tint, the terrace is teeming with visitors enjoying curated cheese boards and wine. At night, Gjusta's patio provides the perfect backdrop for a superb dinner.

Perhaps what makes it stand out most is its devotion to the simple, the fresh, the sustainable, and the locally-sourced. Its perennially busy kitchen is an ode to Southern California—from the warmth of the staff, to the light and buoyant atmosphere, to the symphony of smells coming from behind the counter, to the California sun reflecting on the relaxed interiors.

It shines, not only because of its exceptional coffee and food, but because of its unfaltering devotion to people and community. "Shelley and Fran know all of the employees' names," says Tomas Cruz, a server at Gjusta. "It really is like working with one big family."

Cruz's claim is immediately corroborated when Armistead calls on Artemio Jimenez, whom she has spotted on the other side of the patio, and asks him about his music. Jimenez, a Oaxaca native who also works at Gjusta, plays in a band and hopes to become a music teacher on the weekends.

It seems that Gjusta does it all. It's part bakery, part cafe, part deli, part market, and together, it captures the essence of Venice, rejecting pretension in favor of empathy and intentionality.

For Armistead, though, the concept goes far beyond what can be served on a plate. "[What has been most rewarding about working in this space] is the ability to [focus on a] more circular model of the interconnectivity [within] this industry as it plays into humans, sustainability, impact, art, design, and finance," she explains.

Further inland, Superba Food + Bread is similar.

Much like Gjusta, Superba brings it all back to the ingredients and the people, ignoring convention expectations of what a cafe should be. Equal parts bakery, cafe, and urban park, it has been challenging the status quo since it opened in 2014.

Superba's patio offers a snapshot of its inclusive culture. A plethora of personalities, old and young, commingle in one space, all united by an appreciation for quality and community.

Inside, a baker carefully lays out rows of dough that will eventually become wonderfully crusty baguettes. He works efficiently in a way that only those who have mastered their craft can.

Primarily known for its outstanding bread offerings, it has become, like Gjusta, one of those places that seems to do it all right. During the daytime, there are people casually catching up over brunch, or working on their laptops with a cold brew, or picking up a loaf during a midday break. The tabletops are crowded with glasses of iced coffee sweating under the California sunshine. At nighttime, champagne flutes and wine glasses replace coffee cups and the rush-hour bustle is replaced by dinner's mellow flow.

For locals, Superba has become an intersection between work and leisure. It is, as founder Paul Hibler puts it, "that neighborhood place where we meet on our long walk home together."

Those seeking a similarly all-encompassing cafe experience can find it at the corner of Rose Avenue and Hampton Drive, inside Venice's famous The Rose.

"In its previous [iteration] it was—and still is—[a] neighborhood town square, where people met for meetings, to read a book, for interviews… it was that place that was very casual," says chef and owner Jason Neroni.

Like Gjusta and Superba, The Rose offers something for everyone. "You can have a nice dining experience. You can sit outside and people watch. You can casually read in the back. You can sit [at the bar] and watch the action" says Neroni.

The space itself is an ode to the neighborhood, with walls covered in artwork and photographs by Californian artists like Craig Stecyk, Priscilla Witt, and Pascal Shirley, all playing into the Venetian narrative. It perspires surf, and skate, and funkiness, and is as eclectic as the crowd it serves.

A similarly heterogeneous array of people can be found sipping expertly crafted cups of coffee at Menotti's, a beloved cafe on Windward Avenue, where owner Louie Ryan can typically be spotted mingling with locals on the patio. On this particular Saturday morning, he is joined by his son and Tony Bill, the Oscar-winning

Gjusta

Gjusta

American actor, producer, director, and Venice local.

"[When I look for neighborhoods], I have one stipulation: that they're multicultural and diverse," says Ryan, who chose to settle in Venice Beach for its motley group of visitors and residents.

Unlike Superba, Gjusta, or The Rose, which offer a wide range of food and beverage, Menotti's strictly serves coffee. Named after Italian-born Cesar Menotti, who owned the building in the early decades of the 1900s, Menotti's continues to cater to the local crowd by providing first-rate coffee and a space for connection and community.

"The community is a very big part of it," says Brandon Frank, one of the shop's talented baristas. "Menotti's has been in Venice for eight years or so—it's a coffee community. [Venice] is definitely one of its own—there's a different energy here. But it all comes down to the community."

Gjusta, Superba, The Rose, and Menotti's all have their individual characters and flavors, but they are all united by their mutual dedication to this community. They have, in many ways, developed a symbiotic relationship with the neighborhood and its people that makes it hard to imagine one without the others.

Today, Venice is undergoing yet another transformation. The arrival of tech companies and the surge in commercial venues are inevitably changing the neighborhood's character.

Additionally, the COVID-19 pandemic has also greatly affected the evolution of Venice's cafe culture. But there is, according to Ryan, a silver lining. Terrace dining has proliferated throughout the neighborhood, as tables have spilled onto sidewalks. Streets that were once filled with parked cars now throng with diners and people.

After a period of uncertainty and hardship, the neighborhood seems to be coming back to life in a manner befitting one that has done so several times before.

Journalist and screenwriter Sara Davidson has dubbed Venice a "legendary Phoenix that always seems to rise again from the ashes."

Venice is—and has always been—a place of rebirth, change, individuality, and growth. More than a neighborhood, Venice is a conscious choice to veer away from all things conventional and choose what is unique and extraordinary instead. And in doing so, it promises that whatever comes is better than what came before.
—

# On the Beaches of Los Angeles

WORDS & PHOTOGRAPHS
Pete Milne

On any given day in Manhattan Beach or Hermosa Beach—two of the 15 beaches in the greater Los Angeles area—you can wander up and down the sandy shore and find happy, sunburnt people playing volleyball. From one net to the next you may find a pick-up game just for fun or professional athletes running a structured practice.

But whether "jungle ball" (volleyball played with no rules) or a regulated game, the open community of beach volleyball has a place for you. That's exactly why those nets were put there in the first place.

For decades, beach volleyball has matured into its own culture. Like surfing, anyone and everyone who goes down to the beach to play volleyball can enjoy being a small part of that culture, even for just a day.

Although beach volleyball was first discovered on Waikiki Beach in Honolulu, Hawaii in 1915, the game we know of today has its roots on Santa Monica Beach. As new jetties were being built, vast quantities of sand started to build up, creating wide, open beaches. The residents of Santa Monica were quick to discover these new spaces in the sand for their enjoyment. In no time at all, the first public and permanent volleyball nets were put in place.

First developed in the 1920s, the current format of two players per team (or "doubles"), gained momentum through the Great Depression. It was an affordable activity that provided entertainment, exercise, and a distraction from the worries of life. Even today, it still costs you next to nothing to stroll off the boardwalk with a few friends to an open net and play. And its popularity was reinforced in popular culture by the likes of

The Beatles, who played between shows in 1965, and John F. Kennedy, who brought attention to this sport as a spectator.

April Ross is a local volleyball athlete, whose impressive career has sent her to the Olympics three times, where she earned silver and bronze medals (London and Rio, respectively). In the 2020 Tokyo Olympics, she and her volleyball partner Alix Klineman won gold, making Ross the first woman to have won all three Olympic medals in beach volleyball. A native of California and a national champion while playing indoor volleyball in college, Ross has spent the past 15 years acclimating to playing volleyball on the beach. Over the years, her daily commutes and habits to and from practice put her right in the middle of a culture that is alive and thriving.

"I think the culture on the beach in L.A. is really special. Everyone knows everyone and everyone plays. It's a close-knit community and for the most part, people are really cool. There are tons of courts so you can always find [a] place to set up and play, and you're not going to find better sand anywhere else in California," says Ross.

\*\*\*

Hi-Fi Espresso is a coffee company located in the heart of these beach communities. With three well-designed locations just blocks from the sands of Manhattan, Hermosa, and Redondo beaches, owners Jeff and Karen Prugh have spared no effort in supporting these communities.

"Hermosa is our first location so it's our tried and true baby if you will. The majority of our customers live within walking distance, and walk to us. Which is super cool. There is definitely

a nice merger of specialty coffee, athletics, and the beach. We see an uptick in late spring and summer. I know a lot of the beach players practice straight down from us. We often see a coach meeting his or her players on our back patio, which is awesome." Jeff says.

In the beginning, Hi-Fi Espresso served coffee roasted by Counter Culture. But at the start of the year they've put more attention and focus into roasting their own beans. "Now we're [at] 50/50, offering Counter Culture as our featured roaster and our own beans as well. I think that's the beauty of specialty coffee. People are finding that not all cups of coffee are created equal and are willing to seek that out," Jeff explains

With a passion for coffee, and a mission for community, Hi-Fi Espresso works hand-in-hand to support some of the best athletes that have ever played the game. For April Ross, the benefits of both of these communities are personally experienced.

"One of my favorite things to do on an off day is to go sit and read and/or write at a coffee shop," she says.

"But I don't drink coffee at practice, it can be dehydrating, so I have a cup in the morning and offset it by drinking plenty of water. It is, however, an important part of my morning routine, and stopping at a coffee shop on my way to practice brings me a lot of joy and starts my day off on the right foot."

Being able to have community is extremely important when you're a busy professional athlete and world traveler. The value of having a community such as this can travel with her.

"One of my favorite ways to explore when I'm on the road is to find a coffee shop. I've found some great ones in Europe. New York obviously has some amazing coffee shops. I'll spend hours in these cafes on my days off, it's my way of resetting. I also collect coffee mugs when I travel. They hold the memories of that particular trip and I get to relive them every time I use that mug."

Thanks to the presence of social media, it's becoming easier to see the common ground that April Ross, fellow players, and fans share within these communities across the globe.

"Everyone who takes the game seriously trains in Manhattan or Hermosa Beach (with a few exceptions). If you're just getting started in the sport this is where you need to be," says Ross. "The U.S.A. Volleyball gym is close by and there is always good competition for training."

Mental and physical versatility are equally demanded by this sport, and can take an entire career to learn and perfect. Sometimes the mental wins, sometimes the physical.

But it's not just the human elements that present these unique challenges but the elements of Mother Nature as well. Spending your day on hot sand can be enough to make any athlete doubt their life choices, not to mention the unpredictable wind, or rain. If the weather, mixed with impressive athleticism isn't enough to make this sport truly one-of-a-kind, then the Manhattan Beach Open (MBO) is.

The AVP—Association of Volleyball Professionals, is the nation's largest professional beach volleyball tour. Every year, the tournaments hosted by AVP—from New York City to Austin, Texas, and other cities—represent the sport at the highest level.

But the MBO—the longest-running and most famous volleyball tournament in the history of the sport—is the organization's crown jewel.

"There's a lot of energy at these tournaments and they're sure fun to play in. Everyone really wants to win. If you can manage a title [at Hermosa Beach, or] especially at Manhattan [Beach], it means just a little bit more," says Ross.

Since 1960, the MBO has earned seniority as the "granddaddy" of all tournaments and is celebrated for being the only professional tournament where amateurs can compete for a chance to qualify for the main draw and compete for the title. Although the cash prize for winning this tournament is not to be ignored, the *real* prize is earning an eternal spot on the Manhattan Beach Pier. Inscribed with the names of the winners, the tournament's bronze, volleyball-shaped champion plaques are permanently embedded into the Manhattan Beach Pier.

Always held on the south side of the pier, this weekend tournament comes alive thanks to the 60,000 fans cheering and heckling, which can be quite intense. Sitting courtside listening to the trash-talking can be enough entertainment on its own.

April Ross has won the MBO three times. She knows first-hand what type of competition she faces. "There's a lot on the line at AVP tournaments held in Southern California. The crowds are big. The fans in Southern California really understand beach volleyball so you really have to be on your game."

Food and coffee vendors can be seen throughout the sponsors' tents and announcers' booths that line every inch of space between the boardwalk and the ocean. "Funny enough, the AVP has reached out to us recently regarding the tournaments that are coming up." says Prugh of Hi-Fi Espresso. During long tournament days, from sun-up to sundown, the workers who run them need their fix.

Ross and Klineman, together, dubbed "The A-Team," have ranked #1 in the world and have called South Bay their volleyball home since they first teamed up in 2017. "I only train in L.A. I live an hour south in Orange County, but I do love how the community in Hermosa [Beach] and Manhattan Beach rally around beach volleyball. There are always fun, local tournaments going on and everyone always comes out to the AVP events in the summer. We also always have people stopping by practice and it's usually pretty easy to find teams to play against, or people to help us out at practice. You really feel the support of the community here," said Ross.

As these tournaments slowly began to reappear after taking a hiatus during the COVID-19 pandemic, so did Olympic qualification rounds. As Ross and Klineman prepared for the Tokyo games, these unique beachside communities served as a solid home base for these Olympic champions.

Since beach volleyball was officially introduced as an Olympic sport at the 1996 Summer Olympics in Atlanta, Team U.S.A. has come home with 11 medals, seven of them gold. Having hosted two Olympic summer games—1932 and 1984—Los Angeles will be hosting a third in 2028, the first time since beach volleyball became an Olympic sport. It will be a sweet homecoming for a sport on the very sand that made beach volleyball popular, with the silhouette of the Santa Monica Pier in the distance.
—

# Surfika in Surfurbia

WORDS
Brian Gaffney

PHOTOGRAPHS
Nina Gorbenko

For those familiar with Redondo Beach, a "surfurbia" located in Los Angeles County's South Bay, it should come as no surprise that the city prides itself on presenting novel experiences for its denizens and visitors alike. Redondo Beach hosted the United States' first surfing demonstration by George Freeth, Jr., aka "The Man Who Walked on Water" in 1907, and adopted the Goodyear Airship Columbia as its official bird in 1983. More recently, in 2016, the city added its first single-origin specialty coffee roaster to the list of sites to see.

Incorporated in 1892, Redondo Beach took its name from the land grant Rancho Sausal Redondo ("Ranch of the Round Clump of Willows"). The city and its famous horseshoe-shaped pier are 22 miles southwest of the city of Los Angeles and home to a population of nearly 70,000. Dubbed the "Gem of the Continent" by the "Los Angeles Daily Herald" in 1887, Redondo Beach draws droves of visitors each year for its surfing—some of the best in the country, as evidenced by its mention in The Beach Boys hit song "Surfin' USA"—water sports, beaches, oceanfront dining, and antique and boutique shopping, all while maintaining its classic coastal charm.

Regarding specialty coffee, favorite South Bay shops tend to be independently owned and family operated. A short list includes Dale and Toni Inghram's Smoky Hollow Roasters and Blue Butterfly Coffee Co., named for the endangered El Segundo blue butterfly; Andrew and Natalie Stanisich's Two Guns Espresso, which brought New Zealand's coffee culture to Los Angeles; the Perry family's Klatch Coffee, which highlights varieties, farmers, and specific micro-lots of coffee; and Jeff and Karen Prugh's Hi-Fi Espresso, which employs the powers of coffee and design to kickstart the day, ignite imagination, and inspire creativity.

And then there's Andrés Piñeros's The Boy and the Bear Coffee Roastery, opened January 2016, which offers a deep dive into Colombian coffee culture. Not satisfied to simply serve third wave coffee to Redondo beachers, The Boy and the Bear buys, roasts, and serves coffees from a single origin, Piñeros's home country Colombia, the second largest Arabica coffee producing nation in the world.

Located at the southeast corner of Pacific Coast Highway (PCH) and Carnelian Street, The Boy and the Bear sits across from the restaurant Eat at Joe's, a South Bay landmark, and steps from Redondo Beach's City Hall, public library, and a Whole Foods Market. The building, a conspicuous, all-black, converted furniture store with orange and white lettering, is less than a mile from the Redondo Beach Pier and the Redondo Beach Historic Library, a popular wedding venue. For Piñeros, a punk rock musician and graphic designer, who first came to Los Angeles to study at the Musician's Institute, the cafe and roastery, designed by nearby Long Beach's Camp Design Group, is set to imbue "Colombian coffee from a Colombian owner," supported by a soundtrack of Afro-Colombian percussion and rhythms from the country's Chocó Department. Success, for Andrés, is stimulating his guests' five senses.

Piñeros, who hails from Villavicencio in central Colombia, decided that he would only sell Colombian coffees while steeping himself in the greater Los Angeles coffee scene. By his observation, what was being showcased of Colombian coffees didn't do justice to the world that he'd experienced, explored, and wanted to expose. He says that the shops he visited mostly offered Colombian Supremo (which refers to the bean's size, not its geographic region, farm or producer) or a blend of

Joseph Ramon

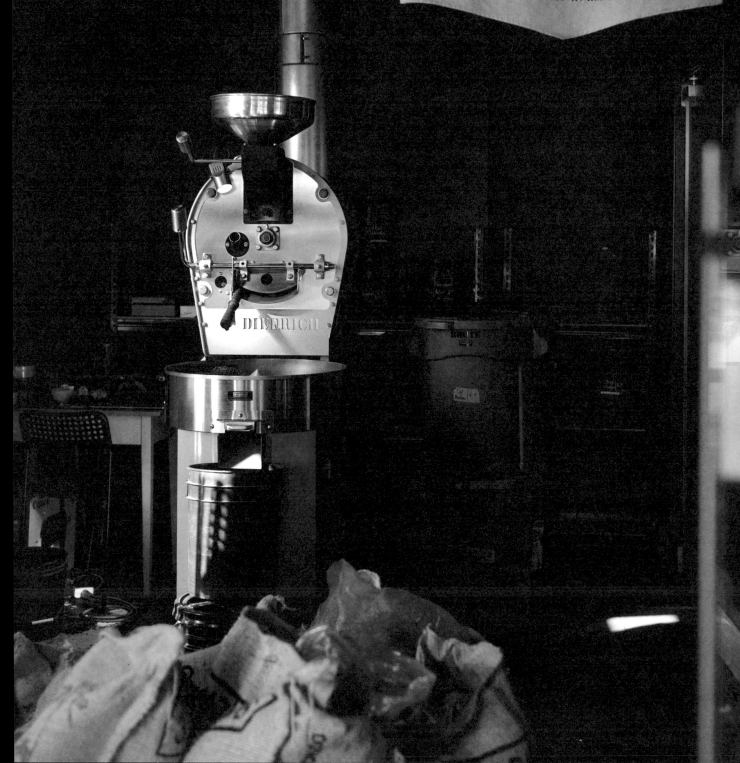

unidentified varietals from unspecified regions. "It became personal" he says, confessing that the limited offering and lack of knowledge pricked his national pride. It was then that he decided to double-down on his commitment to make his employees' and consumers' interactions with Colombian coffee direct and dynamic. His goal was to become the West Coast purveyor of Colombia's best and brightest. (Medellín native Steve Sutton launched Devoción in 2006 and opened its first U.S. cafe and roastery in Brooklyn, New York in 2014 with a similar Colombian coffee farm-to-table model.) Today, The Boy and the Bear sources 70% of its coffees via personal relationships, friends whom Piñeros describes as a "mere WhatsApp message or call away," and sells them to customers who, by his account, are 90% locals.

Hallmarks of the Southern California surfurbian lifestyle are open-mindedness; balance of life, play, and work; and a passion for lived experiences, all of which are greatly influenced by the climatic trifecta of sun, sand, and surf (Redondo Beach's temperature is rarely below 45°F or above 83°F.) Surfers suggest that they strengthen these skills while waiting for the next perfect wave. This leisurely way of life helps to explain the intentional yet informal nature of The Boy and the Bear's consumer coffee education program. The staff is trained in the art of coffee conversation, approached like an open jam session that invites guests to sit-in; meeting them at their current levels of interest and curiosity. Planned programming and formal classes have been replaced with intimate and intuitive interactions among baristas, consumers, and, on occasion, coffee producers—friends visiting from Colombia who come to share, firsthand, with their neighbors to the north, and engage in discussions that emphasize coffee profiles over cupping score points. These direct connections that lead with "honesty and soul" help to make specialty coffee authentic and accessible for everyone, beginners, and connoisseurs alike. Coffee magic strikes when a customer's perception of the coffee matches what they taste in the cup. "When that happens," says Piñeros, "then we all win!"

The metropolis of Los Angeles is known for many things, among them are celebrity and glamor. Alternatively, its surfurbian pockets carry a far different vibe—casual, warm, and carefree. The latter is the spirit of The Boy and the Bear brand that Piñeros wants to bring to Angelenos's specialty coffee culture. More egalitarian than elitist, this South Bay take on the Swedish concept of *fika* (Piñeros lived in Falkenberg, Sweden for four years) is what we describe as "surfika in surfurbia".

Like The Hundred Acre Wood that A.A. Milne's Christopher Robin and Winnie-the-Pooh invited readers to explore, Andrés Piñeros's The Boy and the Bear encourages visitors to survey the South Bay's 90,000 acres fueled by Colombian coffees that are special to all and for all.

—

*Surfurbia is a term coined by architectural critic and writer Reyner Banham in his book, "Los Angeles: The Architecture of Four Ecologies" (1971).

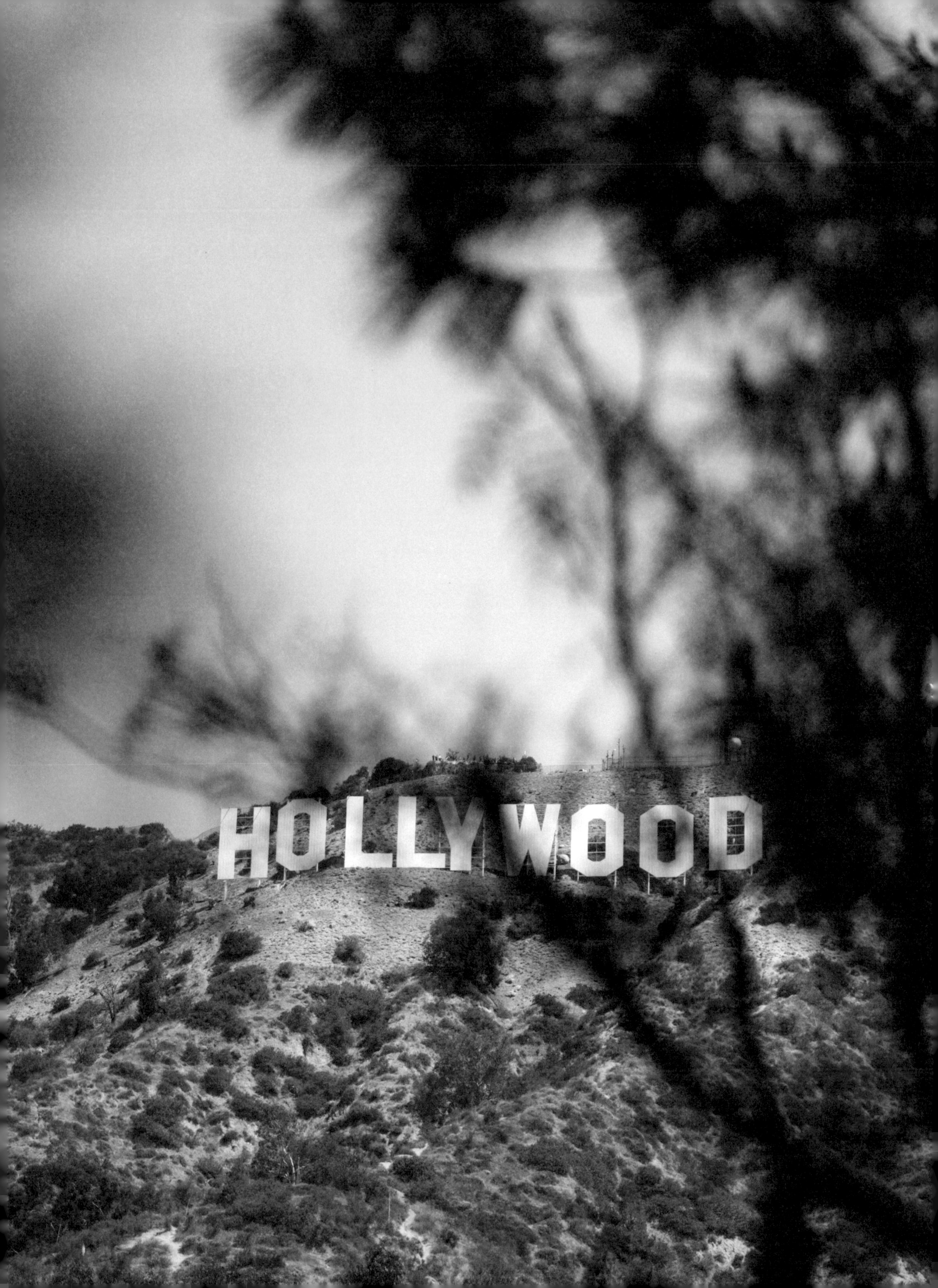
HOLLYWOOD

# Hooray for Hollywood!

WORDS
Faye Bradley

PHOTOGRAPHS
Nina Gorbenko, Daniela Velasco

Hollywood's celebrated 101 Coffee Shop, a 1960s diner, was once the gathering hub for scenes in the movie "Swingers," the HBO series "Entourage" and "Gilmore Girls"—plus it was a celebrity-frequented landmark loved by locals on and off-screen. The iconic coffee joint recently closed permanently due to the COVID-19 pandemic.

Coffee shops have established a long and admirable career in films, from blockbusters like Tarantino's "Reservoir Dogs," filmed at Pat & Lorraine's, to the indie 1997 chick flick "Romy and Michele's High School Reunion," filmed inside Swingers (the name of the movie was inspired by this diner). This emblem of daily life—the art of coffee—is represented in many forms, from the director's creative process to shooting on set, to the popularity of certain venues based on celebrity sightings. Hollywood is the beating heart for film in Los Angeles, where the intersection of movies and independent coffee culture has surged in recent years, creating a new wave of artisan coffee spots—and inspiration for directors.

In the 50s and 60s, when coffee was depicted in a European setting, it was associated with sophistication, an image reinforced by glamorous movie stars like Audrey Hepburn and Princess Grace Kelly, who sipped espresso in Rome, or the Côte d'Azur. Whereas in America, coffee drinking scenes would take place more frequently in diners. Although this portrayal is still present in film, the grassroots movement in Hollywood has brought more independent coffee shops to the scene, thanks to the unique atmosphere and creative allure—plus, people are willing to support these businesses. "They are usually more attentive and can give educated answers about their coffee, where it comes from and their process," Gabe Sachs, the director who filmed "90210" and "Diary of a Wimpy Kid," told us. Undeniably, Hollywood has changed too. "When David Simon of Kilroy [a real estate investment company] discussed how they wanted to bring Hollywood back to Hollywood a decade ago, I was interested in being part of that transition," Jean Shim, founder and CEO of Rubies+Diamonds, a chic coffee shop on Sunset Boulevard, told us. "He brought in a big studio, Viacom, to Columbia Square and Netflix came in soon after. I used to work at the CNN building 30-plus years ago and remember how vibrant it was. And then everyone left for the Westside. It's nice to see Hollywood come back."

Coffee shops in Hollywood have added to its plethora of mid-century diners with independent venues catering to the global third wave coffee movement. Blackwood Coffee Bar, a coffee shop that incorporates vintage interiors and photography, witnessed the explosion of high-quality caffeine in Hollywood. "I think coffee plays a really important social role in Hollywood," said founder Keith Wixson, "One of the reasons people come to coffee shops [in Hollywood] is to see other people, be seen themselves, and to potentially have an unexpected and spontaneous experience."

To Sachs, meeting at a coffee shop takes the pressures off Hollywood work and social culture in business meetings. "When someone wants to grab a coffee to discuss work or an idea or wants thoughts on their projects, I feel like a coffee shop provides a more open, creative atmosphere." Moreover, coffee shops in shows are a great way to get to know your characters outside their work environments, but sometimes you can get to know them on a coffee break, he added. "We created the NBC drama 'The Night Shift,' and during stressful shifts [in the show], [the characters] would often head to the break room

and grab a coffee. It's a great atmosphere [for] heart-to-heart discussions and [learning] more about your characters." The director added that he shot a few scenes for "90210" at Peach Pit in Beverly Hills.

The most popular coffee scenes featured in iconic Hollywood films are filmed at old-school diners rather than actual coffee shops—and sadly, many of them are closed. Johnie's, established in 1956, was known for its futuristic Googie design, making it the perfect, retro backdrop for "The Big Lebowski" and "Reservoir Dogs." Then there's "Valley Girl" at Du-par's Studio City, where Randy, played by a young Nicolas Cage, falls in love with a punk girl on the "wrong side of Hollywood." Legendary Hollywood restaurant Musso & Frank was featured in Tim Burton's "Ed Wood," a story about a director outcast, and sets the scene for Wood (Johnny Depp) to meet Orson Welles (Vincent D'Onofrio). The coffee spot was also used for "Citizen Kane." Mel's Coffee Shop is also a household name in Hollywood, used as a feature location by George Lucas in his 1973 film "American Graffiti" and in a scene of 1967 film "Guess Who's Coming to Dinner" with Spencer Tracy and Katharine Hepburn.

Decades later, films and TV shows are seeing new coffee shops cropping up in scenes, in part due to the paradigm shift in Hollywood coffee culture. "We've shot TV episodes for both Amazon and Netflix within the past few months," said Kian Abedini, founder of Compelling Coffee, an independent coffee shop that started as a pop-up in downtown L.A. (now in Hollywood Hills). In March 2021, Oscar-nominated "Promising Young Woman," featuring Carey Mulligan, tells the tale of a woman working at a coffee shop in L.A. Although the story wasn't filmed at a real coffee shop, Universal Pictures Home Entertainment organized a collaboration with four female-owned Hollywood/L.A. coffee shops, including The Palm Coffee Bar, Lavender & Honey Espresso Bar, The Assembly Cafe, and Romancing The Bean, to curate pop-ups around the city to honor Mulligan's character Cassie with her story and love for coffee. Each venue featured themed coffee merchandise and specialty beverages in anticipation of the film. Shi Jun Ng, owner of The Assembly Cafe, told us that "Coffee feels like a cornerstone for our West Hollywood community and their daily life—the majority of our customers come daily as part of their routine." Showcasing coffee culture in film is important, he noted. "Hopefully, through viewing it on screen, people will in turn be more willing to expand the breadth and variety of their coffee experience. That, I believe, creates opportunities for the myriad small, specialty coffee establishments—much like ours— to sustainably thrive in the long term." The venue is currently planning pop-ups across L.A. before re-assessing a future brick-and-mortar.

Alfred Coffee on Melrose Place has become a hot spot for filming in recent years and is well known for its cult celebrity following and monthly coffee sleeve collaborations—boasting partnerships with the likes of Disney, Netflix, Kylie Cosmetics, and Bumble. "We had a hilarious episode of 'Curb Your Enthusiasm' filmed at Brentwood; an episode of 'Ballers' at Melrose Place; and 'Keeping Up With The Kardashians' at several locations around town," said Josh Zad, Founder and CEO. "Not too long ago, the only option for finding specialty coffee in Hollywood was the typical tourist trap, whose only selling point was organic Italian-roast coffee," said Abedini, "Now that L.A. as a city is a little more into specialty coffees with the idea of terroir, there are some great options all around." Compelling Coffee has also been featured in recent films and shows. "One of the shows

is a very well-known British police drama," he said, "I can say that different directors want different things—one production loved the way our patio seating looked, another wanted a close-up shot of someone ordering at our counter—we have a unique terrazzo order counter—and another wanted a shot of someone speaking against our plant wall. Generally, I've found that productions want an upscale atmosphere with clean, minimal branding, but with some kind of unique feature."

"Movies and TV have the unique ability to capture specific moments in time," Zad explained, "It's important to highlight coffee culture in film to show future generations what life was like in our moment of time." Interestingly, this highlights the increase in boutique coffee shops represented in film—but also the trends in consumer behaviors. "Film also influences human acts and tracks what is currently trending—we are seeing more and more shows and movies featuring characters drinking boba or referencing oat milk, which depict the ever-evolving coffee culture our world is experiencing." At Compelling Coffee, ingredients are sourced through a local food program that works with Hollywood Farmer's Market a couple of blocks away. "Specialty coffee has thankfully grown past the point where we call our baristas "nerds" and do the whole stereotype about consumers and professionals being snobs, so I think it's really important to avoid showing that."

Besides coffee's role in film, Hollywood culture extends to offscreen routines integrated by celebrities, filmmakers, and residents. "Whether we're on our way to the office, headed to a film shoot, or treating ourselves with a latte before we start to work at home, coffee is how we get going," said Abedini, "We've been lucky to have been featured in a few film shoots since opening, and so directors, scouts, and film crews stop in all the time—as well as one of my all-time favorite actors." Celebrity sightings often happen after their gym sessions or if they are in the area. "L.A. is a town full of movers and shakers. If you're not grabbing a coffee on the way to your next meeting, you're looking for a chill patio to hang out with a friend, colleague, or client (over coffee, of course)," added Zad, "L.A. culture revolves around this single beverage as a way to connect with others, while also helping fuel the hustling lifestyle Angelenos are known for." Alfred's Studio City location is close to CBS Studios which often brings in major film crew orders. "Many actors, producers, directors, and celebrities come into Rubies+Diamonds because of our special drink coconut sea salt cold brew," said Shim. "Some drive an hour to get to the store to have this drink—it also helps that we have many studios in the area that bring in everyone from the entertainment industry." "My favorite celebrity experience, though, was when an Academy Award-nominated actress camped out at a corner table and filled out her holiday cards—I knew then that we had created a really comfortable and welcoming space," said Wixson.

Coffee runs are also massively important in the behind-the-scenes process. Andy Macat, who is part of a Hollywood camera department, shared with us his experiences. "Most of the time on a movie set, if you are working in a location near a coffee shop, the head of your department will hand you their credit card and ask for you to take everyone's order," he said. "It's a nice gesture. [You'll need] to borrow a golf cart to transport the 15-20 coffee [orders]." Remembering bosses' favorite orders makes a strong impression and it's part of the everyday experience on set. Shim told us that although she is in the coffee industry, her passion and background are also in filmmaking. "Coffee and filmmakers go hand in hand. On set, if you have great coffee, you have a happy crew," she said, "Filmmakers use coffee shops as their meeting place to discuss their projects too."

"We get a really interesting mix of creative folks who work in film, TV, music, fashion, and comedy," added Wixson, "What I didn't expect, but came to really enjoy, is that different people would unexpectedly run into each other at Blackwood and end up staying and start collaborating—our Sunset Boulevard location organically became this creative hub."

"Coffee is an integral part of daily life for so many, so it's natural for the film industry to weave those storylines into movies and TV," said Zad, "The intimacy of the spaces, with the clanking of the grinders and humming of the espresso steam in the background, lend themselves very well to film."
—

Kian Abedini, Compelling Coffee

# Milking It:
# L.A.'s Alternative Milk Scene

Words
Imogen Lepere

PHOTOGRAPHS
Adam Goldberg, Daniela Velasco

Walk into any supermarket in America and the non-dairy milk aisle is overflowing: almond, oat, coconut, pea, hemp, cashew—if you can imagine it, chances are a health company somewhere is milking it.

It's hard to believe that pre-2008 alternative milks were limited to commercial Silk brand soy milk and dusty bottles of long-life rice milk buried on the top shelf in health food shops. The entire industry pretty much just served vegans and those with lactose allergies. Fast forward 14 years and it's safe to say that America is in the midst of a white gold rush. According to a new study by Morning Consultant, 67% of U.S. adults have tried a non-dairy milk, with roughly 1 in 3 slurping it at least once a week.

Alternative milks' environmental credentials have played a large part in their broadening appeal in recent years. According to a University of Oxford study, producing a single glass of dairy milk every day for a year requires 7,000 sq. ft. of land (the same as two tennis courts), which is more than 10 times than needed for producing the same amount of oat milk.

Vance Lehmkuhl from the American Vegan Society believes that Americans are moving away from milk because of a lack of trust in the dairy industry, as well as health concerns. "Non-dairy milks offer great nutrition (varying from product to product) that's free of cholesterol and hormones, lower in saturated fat, and uncontaminated by residue from the milking process."

Given its proud wellness culture, it is perhaps little surprise that California is leading the charge in the non-dairy milk revolution. The Golden State has contributed a platoon of brands including New Barn Organics, Westsoy, and Ripple Foods. However in L.A., cafes are now opting to make their own, treating it as a

Orange latte with hazelnut milk, Ten

specialty item on the menu in its own right rather than a mere add on.

One of the city's earliest adopters of house-made alternative milk was Bar Nine, an exposed-beam, concrete-floor space in Culver City. "When I was writing the business plan for Bar Nine back in 2012 I spent most of my afternoons off, roasting coffee on my sample roaster and also playing around with different non-dairy milks," says founder Zayde Naquib. "I kept coming back to the simplicity of hazelnut milk. The taste was distinctive but it had a mellowness that allowed the coffee to shine through and was also really juicy on the finish, whereas a lot of raw nut milks can be dry or astringent."

Naquib now makes hazelnut milk fresh every morning and says that about 40% of customers order it instead of dairy, with some making trips especially for it. "It became such a staple at Bar Nine that we'll be introducing it at our new cafe Ten, imminently due to popular demand. I personally enjoy it the most in an iced latte, though it is pretty [fabulous] with our house rooibos chai too."

Over in Larchmont, the rich, creamy almond-macadamia milk at Charles Babinski and Kyle Glanville's Go Get Em Tiger has become something of an urban legend. This ever buzzing bar serves excellent coffee, but has become best known for a quirky signature drink called the Business & Pleasure: a three-part beverage consisting of an espresso shot, a palate cleanser of sparkling tea, and finally, a mix of espresso, syrup, and almond-macadamia milk. Now that'll get you going.

Another blended dairy alternative that has been making a splash in the city's coffee scene is the unsweetened, organic almond and pumpkin seed milk served at Honey Hi. This sunshiney spot in Echo Park was founded by best friends Kacie Carter, a nutritionist, and Caitlin Sullivan in 2016 and is known as much for it's friendly atmosphere as the feel-good food that streams out of the kitchen from breakfast through to late lunch. Alternative milk here is treated with the same philosophy as any other dish on the menu: it's gluten- and refined sugar-free and made with ingredients sourced from local farmer's markets. Try it with coffee roasted by Canyon Coffee or in signature drinks that promise a host of health benefits, such as the Mushroom Dandy Brew (roasted dandelion coffee alternative with chaga mushrooms).

Like so many great things in life, alternative milk has its downsides too. Ryan Fisher, Head of Coffee Buying and Roasting at Santa Monica's Goodboybob, says: "The main challenge is that alternative milks don't always work well with coffee. Acidity presents differently with nut milks, which can lead to curdling if suddenly overheated. You really have to understand the dynamic between the milk and the particular type of coffee you're using." Fisher and his team have spent hours perfecting that craft and now their housemade non-dairy milks account for 40% of sales. "Almond milk makes up about 25% and oat 15%, but in the last year I've noticed a lot of people switching to oat, perhaps because producing almonds takes so much water."

As any latte-lover or cappuccino convert knows, no coffee is complete without a layer of fluffy foam. And this is another challenge that baristas must overcome, particularly if they want to make latte art: non-dairy milks are not born equal in terms of froth potential. Soy has a stretch that's similar to dairy, which is why it has been such a favorite for so long, while others, such as rice milk, don't have enough protein to achieve the required fluff.

"It's important to be mindful of fat content to get the texture you're looking for when steaming," says Naquib. "Hazelnuts are pretty fatty nuts, so they can be closer to steaming dairy on their own, as opposed to something like oat, which while delicious, requires the addition of oil or another fat source to steam properly."

Despite the challenges, Naquib believes house-made alternative milk is here to stay: "I believe there will be a future where dairy gets dropped from menus altogether. Non-dairy alternatives have gotten better and better and they represent a far more sustainable future." With so many benefits, one feels there is little point crying over the fact that dairy milk may be spilt for good.
—

# Gold River

WORDS
Duncan Nielsen

PHOTOGRAPHS
Adam Goldberg, Daniela Velasco

The vibes in Los Angeles can get pretty crossed up. Like the some 10,000 billboards that pockmark the freeways and boulevards, they all hum in your head, clamoring for attention at every level of the sun-soaked psyche. But between the ham-handed megalomania of the movie biz, the New Age mysticism, witchcraft, and woo woo percolating from the seams of modern Los Angeles life, there is a subtly churning power, a decidedly chic caffeine-fueled current seeking to provide balance and comfort to newcomers, long-time residents, and visitors alike.

Central to that current is Echo Park–based Canyon Coffee, a roaster founded in 2016 on L.A.'s Westside by partners Ally Walsh and Casey Wojtalewicz. In both aesthetic and ethos, the company plays off a Mother Earth mood board shared by local retailers—places like Christy Dawn, a farm-to-closet women's clothier, and General Store, which sells bone-toned home goods and salt-of-the-earth knicknacks—to create a sense of shared soil. But even as Canyon resonates in tandem with modern handicrafts, or the boho chic and cottagecore movements, it has a unique style and voice.

"Ally and I met in Beachwood Canyon, we had the idea to start our company in Rivas Canyon, and we were in Temescal Canyon where we would hike almost daily when the name [for our business] occurred to us," says Wojtalewicz. "Just as coffee brings people together, canyons clearly felt like places where people, energies, and ideas converge."

He and Walsh also took multiple visits to Georgia O'Keeffe's home near Abiquiu, New Mexico, which frames vignettes of the high desert and canyon lands that surround it. From the outset, a naturalist theme was mounting to replace the greasy "mustache and motorcycle vibe," as Walsh coins it, that had had its day through the 2010s.

The refreshing perspective brought on by jaunts through the Southwest's hinterlands and L.A.'s parks is accounted for in Canyon's packaging. On a simple brown bag, a white label created by Los Angeles–based designer Fred L'Ami features a gold foil line elegantly winding its way from top right to bottom left, representing a river cutting into a canyon. The geological feature evokes L.A.'s myriad hiking trails in its canyons; you can almost get a whiff of the sycamores and chaparral. Behind each label are certified-organic roasts from the broader coffee belt, and each carries a regionally inspired name printed in relaxed and reclining italic font.

Canyon found its footing amid the quotidian paces of L.A. life by showing up to places where designers and makers converge. Walsh, a model, and Wojtalewicz, a musician, both long-acquainted with gig life, would serve drinks at Echo Park Craft Fair alongside reclaimed-rattan brokers and tasteful textiles. They'd show up to Mercado Sagrado (or, Sacred Market), another annual fair substantiated with more one-off events throughout the year that are all "designed to inspire a more connected, conscious way of living." Everything with a grain of salt, but when Canyon arrives as a promoted post in your Instagram feed, know that they never hid behind the vapid digitalia of social media.

While we wait for an official Canyon Coffee storefront, those navigating the greater Los Angeles area can get a taste of what they're up to at an array of brick and mortars. Find their roasts at Neighborhood in La Brea, a shop Walsh and Wojtalewicz

Casey Wojtalewicz & Ally Walsh by Justin Chung

Canyon Coffee at Neighborhood Coffee

helped brothers Matthew and Darin Friedman open in 2019. The shop trades the connectivity of Wi-Fi for that of *fika*, the daily Swedish practice of connecting with family, friends, or colleagues over a bite or a drink. If you're in the Highland Park area, you can pair one of Canyon's roasts with the paleo pancakes or a ranchero egg pot at Amara Kitchen. Or, head to 6IXTHSENSE in Koreatown for a blue-colored drink called the Malibu Latte, or just get an iced pour over made with Canyon's Ethiopan beans.

For those looking to replenish their *juju*, Moon Juice in Echo Park offers a space-age wellness menu that includes adaptogen-rich chocolate chaga donuts, and something called "sex dust," which Canyon once blended into espresso drinks to the delight of attendees at the Mercado Sagrado.

In a town that wears many faces, Walsh and Wojtalewicz have managed to create something as comforting to locals as it is welcoming to strangers, which is a result of their own experiences out on the road. "I was in Portland, Maine, doing a job," says Walsh, before explaining how she'd often be subjected to jugs of corporate coffee that had been sitting way too long. "I like to look for local roasters, and I found Tandem Coffee—it was in an old converted gas station, and everyone was so nice and the coffee was so good," she says. For Walsh, it was a moment of solace—a heartwarming and authentic feeling.

For Wojtalewicz, a musician who's spent his share of weeks and months touring the world and far away from his own bed, finding coffee in each new town provided a deep breath between the dull hum of the open road and noisy nightclub life. "It was the last show of the tour," says Wojtalewicz, remembering a moment of satori at Treasure Island Music Fest in San Francisco in 2013. "I had a bad meal, and was just really not doing great," he laughs. "It was sunset, which was so beautiful over the bay, and Sightglass was making a pour over backstage. It was just amazing—it saved me."

Back in L.A., Canyon's founders continue to pay forward moments like these. They've woven each of their individual experiences into the coffee they roast, creating an intentional throughline shared by the designers, makers, and craftspeople with whom they surround themselves. It's an unfiltered, handmade scene that gives us more than a few reasons to find our balance in a well-made cup of coffee.

—

Verve Roastery Del Sur

# Welcome Space

WORDS
Chérmelle D. Edwards

PHOTOGRAPHS
Adam Goldberg, Daniela Velasco

Before the third wave of coffee arrived, coffee shops were just four walls with ample seating, and a roaster hidden out of sight. Now, coffee shop owners increasingly work with designers to create spaces that combine function with beauty.

Los Angeles, the largest city in California, gives coffee drinkers more than meets the cup with its specialty coffee shops. Increasingly, there's a design emphasis on the point where coffee workers interact with the customer: the coffee bar. Its physical construction not only visually defines a coffee shop, but perhaps more importantly, how people move in and around the space and interact with each other.

In 2007, Verve Coffee Roasters opened on 41st Avenue in Santa Cruz, California. Fifteen years and 14 coffee shops later, its founders Colby Barr and Ryan O'Donovan have established a visual style that informs the guest experience within its spaces. In particular, its downtown Los Angeles Arts District location, Roastery Del Sur, which opened in August 2019, exemplifies Los Angeles's historical, mid-century design heritage. The designers at Design Bitches remained faithful to that design aesthetic, using natural materials and bathing the space with natural light.

Roastery Del Sur has the intimacy of a Japanese *kissaten*—Verve has four locations in Japan—and one perceives this location intends to create spaces within a space. The register, made of white oak and designed like a mid-century modern credenza, functions like a concierge desk. It's a welcoming point from which guests scatter to explore different areas: the standing bar adjacent to the roasting room; the conversation pit with low-slung tables and plush seating; or to the second level, which gives you an overview of it all.

"We have always been about putting the process right up in front of people and doing all that we can to remove the barrier between ourselves and our customers. [Since the opening of our first store] in 2007, we tried to build low countertops and remove any commercial 'back of house' elements from [view]. We want people to feel more like they are in a kitchen or living space than in some commercial facility," said Barr.

With a bar that has multiple destinations in one, the existing and created light of Roastery Del Sur is like an open invitation to coexist among its illuminated lines and converging angles. No design choice goes unnoticed here, including the olive tree that was selected after scouring a dozen Southern California nurseries. As it gives air and life to the ritual of coffee, so does the design of Roastery Del Sur, which contributes to "this leading edge of coffee we all are a part of [and] is still just beginning," says Barr. "Los Angeles is definitely not just another city, it's almost incomparable, actually."

Moving northwest to Silverlake, a 1,040 square-foot coffee shop named Dinosaur Coffee opened in December 2014 by then-owners Michelle and Ben Hantoot. Once an audio music equipment repair store, the shop is a product of MASS Architecture & Design and builder Robert Canas. Wood slots in the shape of a dinosaur's bones hover over a wide-open bar along with the menu, bordered by curved lines along its wall. This setup makes the production of a cup of coffee as transparent as the see-through pastry case, which is framed by black and white ceramic tile and juxtaposed by a cherry-red La Marzocco espresso machine.

Dinosaur's dynamic bar design was a huge factor in Janine and Saadat Awan's decision to take ownership of the space in October 2020, "the size, circular shape, and central placement of the bar draws customers in and creates an organic flow of service," says Janine Awan. "It's akin to a performance stage, no matter where you go, you have to glance over to see what's exactly going on."

The space has been thoughtfully designed to do more than just flirt with your eyes. Perhaps, more importantly, it endeavors to invite you into a relationship with coffee and linger for a while.

Thirty miles south in Newport Beach are Kyle Kennelly and Rebecca Mantei, who spent the winter of 2016 turning a warehouse into Daydream Surf Shop. The two, along with a host of family and friends built out this specialty coffee and surf shop with their hands.

On a freezing night in December, the bar, which is made out of steel, was welded together using materials they bought on a microscopic budget, says Mantei. She created bar sketches wherein she envisioned a rainbow shape, "there's something about the absence of hard angles that is inherently softer, and I think more inviting. You can flow around the bar without running into a hard edge."

The crescent curve is reinforced by steel slab lengths that are sectioned into three zones. Each zone is a different height and offers a different kind of interaction with the barista, the coffee, or a different experience sitting at the bar.

Simple pine plywood from Home Depot gives the space a light-colored wood interior that helps offset the Southern California heat. Space is ample here. "We want every part of the shop to be visible from any point in the space and keep your attention closer to ground level so that there is a lot of airspace above you... kind of like a thinking room so to speak. The symbolism here is that visibility represents transparency, we wanted a space that worked with people and vendors who value transparency as well as holding that as a core value for Daydream too," said Kennelly.

A city that has, at times, overpopulated some neighborhoods with coffee shops while leaving others behind, Los Angeles offers a plethora of coffee experiences. In the centrally located West Adams neighborhood, you'll find coffee among historical buildings and a population dominated by people of color, who have bolstered this community for over a century with their culture and dollars. Opened in 2018 on a main thoroughfare, Highly Likely, helmed by partners Alex Matthews, Chelsea Matthews, and Cary Mosier, was custom-designed by Klein Agency, which drew inspiration from coffee shops in Australia and Mexico.

Somewhat inspired by the fluidity of a skate ramp, the bar at Highly Likely sits front and center when the cafe's roller doors open. It is acutely shaped, with a short curve that takes advantage of its center placement, giving it a merry-go-round feel, a carousel that features goodies—everything from Pocky to Lumen hemp shots and hot sauce. "It celebrates the heartbeat of our goods," says Matthews.

Globe lights drop over the bar, adding accent lighting to an already well-lit space. "It was just as simple as knowing that we wanted to create a design element through lighting, and tracing it across the bar felt needed and natural. It gives the space a soft glow in the evenings, when all the natural light that generally floods in dips below the coast," said Matthews.

Los Angeles, a sunlit city, whose basin is perfumed with ocean air and framed by palm tree-lined streets, is home to a rising class of coffee shops that are reimagining the spaces they inhabit. Proprietors who understand that a coffee bar isn't just a coffee bar in Los Angeles are transforming their corners into a welcoming place along this coastal drift.

—

# Roasting Our Way to Community and Diversity

WORDS
Sabrina Sucato

PHOTOGRAPHS
Chérmelle D. Edwards

As a beverage, coffee knows no bounds. It's enjoyed in some form or another across the globe, with preparations as myriad as the individuals behind them. In Los Angeles, its inherent diversity shines not only through how it's made, but also through those who prepare it. After all, a proper cup of coffee is like a snowflake; no two brews are exactly alike.

And neither are the roasters who power them.

At Seven Syllables Coffee in Cerritos, roasting is all about community and camaraderie. The online-based roastery is helmed by Roscoe Aquilo and Tim Hasta, two Filipino Americans whose business partnership had nothing to do with coffee and everything to do with music, their other passion. Both were in a band called Seven Syllables Spoken, so, when they reconvened after respective stints at second wave coffee shops, they decided to keep the name as a nod to how they met. Today, Seven Syllables is a roastery and retail coffee company known for its ever-changing blends. Within the Los Angeles community, its presence as a BIPOC-owned and operated business further diversifies a broadening cultural landscape.

"I think L.A. has always been full of culture," Aquilo notes. "It's an amazing thing to see so many people of different cultures creating spaces for the coffee community. Coffee shops used to be seen as a sign of gentrification, and I think the BIPOC community has sort of taken the power back while providing service to their own communities."

That appreciation for the local coffee community extends to Woodcat and Dinosaur, two Los Angeles coffee shops owned by Saadat Awan and his wife Janine. After moving to Echo Park and discovering a lack of specialty coffee in the area in 2012,

Tony (Tonk) Konecny & Sumi Ali, Yes Plz

Jamil Radney, The Reverse Orangutan

the couple channeled their respective backgrounds in coffee and architecture and in graphic design and branding into two go-to shops serving house-roasted coffee in the city.

Of Woodcat and Dinosaur's presence in the community, Awan observes, "There are a lot of terrific POC- and woman-owned coffee shops here, frequented by widely diverse groups of people, ours included." While this is a relatively new development—such a diverse, specialty coffee scene did not exist when Awan moved to the city—Awan has hope that it will flourish.

"If the pandemic has taught us in the coffee world one thing, it's that specialty coffee is still, for the most part, a widely accessible and sought after commodity," he says. "It's taught us that if things seem hard, maybe a simple cup of coffee and a nod from your neighborhood barista will make things okay, if only for one moment."

That notion of accessibility extends to The Reverse Orangutan, a coffee company named after a chess move. With cafes and a roastery in Claremont, Glendora, and Pomona, the business is a partnership between owners Geoff Clark and Jamil Radney, who met while working at Dripp and Espresso Republic. Each having worked in the industry for more than a decade, the duo joined forces to craft artisan roasts, not to mention homemade syrups and sauces, with intent. Yet beyond this dedication to top-level coffee, The Reverse Orangutan also stands out as a business that emphasizes diversity.

"I think it's fair to say that in my neck of the woods, I am the token Black coffee shop," observes Radney. "In my tenure of cafes or specialty food that I've worked in, I've usually been the only Black male in the company, only to be accompanied by—maybe one or two at the most—Black female coworkers. We have a diverse crew at our cafe, from age, orientation, gender, and ethnicity. I'm proud of that. With that said, I'm not here typecasting baristas, so we can only be as diverse as candidates have interest."

To his point, promoting diversity within the coffee industry is a give-and-take that requires the cooperation of businesses and customers. Only when those two harmonize can a greater sense of inclusion be achieved. Even so, as Radney points out, that's only part of the process when it comes to developing a more diverse coffee culture.

"If we want to see an evolution of inclusion and diversity, we must first enfranchise our fellow Americans to be able to use the voice that has been purposefully muzzled since our emancipation, terrorized through our civil movements, and bottlenecked through our pragmatism that if the moral arc is to bend towards justice that we must live to fight another day so we can bend that arc," he says. "With all of that said—and I know it's a lot—watching Black entrepreneurs succeed in our society is always an inspiration to me as they are building ladders to bring up our community."

Back in central Los Angeles, Yes Plz channels that forward-thinking inspiration as it dives headlong into its direct-to-consumer coffee business, along with people like Tohm Ifergan of Dayglow Coffee, who focuses on mail-order subscription services, which helped his business weather the pandemic when his two coffee shops in the city were closed. Led by Tony (Tonx) Konecny, an industry mainstay who sold his eponymous Tonx Coffee to Blue Bottle in 2014, and Sumi Ali, a barista

extraordinaire who honed his skills at Sqirl's G&B pop-up, Yes Plz aims to make each subscription unique. Releases are one-time only and usually custom blends, since, as Konecny notes, "We embrace this kind of heretical idea that there isn't a single origin coffee that can't be made at least a little better with some judicious blending."

Notably, this notion of artful blending establishes a parallel between the beans themselves and the industry as a whole.

"L.A. is one of the most diverse cities in the U.S., and I think the coffee culture here is starting to reflect that a lot more, on both sides of the counter and in who is owning and operating shops, so that's been great to watch happen," Konecny observes. As he, along with Aquilo and Radney, points out, while the evolution is underway, it is not complete. Instead, the journey toward a diverse industry remains a work in progress, one that walks the line between creativity and competition in an attempt to form new blueprints.

"The conversation around gentrification often singles out hip coffee shops, and often for good reasons," Konecny notes. "It's going to take a lot of new thinking and intention around what a brick and mortar business should be and who is being represented. I'm optimistic that the post-COVID era sees more new ideas taking root, and a lot of pent-up creativity blossoming." —

Sadaat & Janine Awan, Dinosaur Coffee

# Best in Show:
# L.A.'s Canine-Friendly Coffee Shops

WORDS
Imogen Lepere

PHOTOGRAPHS
Daniela Velasco

Sure coffee shops need walk-ins, particularly in a city with rent prices like L.A. But no cafe can survive on strangers alone. Regulars are what keep them afloat, both financially and emotionally. What is a coffee shop without the locals the whole team knows by name; the best friends who always stop by on their morning walk; the favorite customer who regularly chills out on the terrace? We're talking about furry regulars rather than human ones here, although naturally they tend to come as a pair.

The U.S. has the highest domestic dog, cat, and bird populations in the world and the pandemic has only reinforced this. In its latest study, the American Pet Products Association reported that 11.38 million U.S. households have welcomed a new animal friend since the start of the pandemic. And who can blame them? The positive impacts on mental health from having a dog in your life have been well documented and, with the rise in those working from home, pet ownership is now a viable option for many more people.

Legislation under the California Health and Safety Code bars dogs from establishments that serve food. But since 2011, cafe owners have had the option of opening their outdoor space to pups. While not all cafes in L.A. are dog-friendly, those that are provide dog owners with a safe haven, where they can sip specialty coffee and find some inspiration while their pup enjoys some fresh air.

Jasmine Poulton is an actor and writer who recently moved to Franklin Hills with her rescued terrier mix Jimi. Although they love exploring the neighborhood's hills and hidden staircases, their favorite activity is going for coffee at Muddy Paw in Silverlake, which donates a percentage of its proceeds to canine charities. "They have a lovely patio in the back, which is designed for both dogs and humans, so Jimi and I can sit for hours while he says 'hi' to other pups. The seating is really comfy and I find the energy there equally calm and stimulating, perfect for writing."

Of all L.A.'s dog-friendly cafes, Muddy Paw is leading the pack in terms of facilities. The terrace has wall hooks for securing leashes, and the Eagle Rock location even has a fenced in dog park where pups can socialize while their owners work or do some socializing themselves. Quality is a buzzword here. Canine cupcakes and macaroons are sourced from Bubba Rose, an all-natural treat brand, while coffee is roasted at co-owner Darren LaBorie's family roastery, Port City Coffee Roasters, which has been going for more than 25 years.

Natalie Aldacour-La Borie, who runs the cafe alongside her husband Darren, says it was their own furry family that inspired the joint: "We have three dogs, all rescues: Abby (pug and beagle mix), Santana (shar-pei and labrador mix), and Maple (boxer and pitbull mix). A lot of cafes in L.A. call themselves dog-friendly but we kept finding that when we got there there wasn't really enough space for dogs and humans to relax. Many of them are just seats on busy sidewalks, which is very difficult for dogs as there is so much traffic. So we designed Muddy Paw to have everything that we wished had been on offer for our babies—individual water bowls, safe play areas, plenty of shade."

As any dog (and human) knows, even if a cafe describes itself as dog-friendly, that doesn't guarantee a warm welcome and no one likes to feel as if their presence is merely being tolerated, which is why Doubting Thomas is an excellent choice for canine coffee breaks. It's a long, whitewashed space in Historic Filipinotown filled with mismatched furniture and the smell of

Derek Klamerus with Marty, Destroyer

freshly baked pastries stuffed with whatever fruit owner Natalie Shim has found at the farmer's market that week. The terrace is well-shaded, the water bowl refreshed regularly, and her team members are all certified dog-lovers.

When he isn't making specialty pour over coffee, head barista Robert Mayes is walking down the line, which can stretch around the corner of Temple Street, saying hello to every dog he passes. "We have the most diverse patronage I've ever seen, which is the number one reason I love working here. Every guest is completely unique and that goes for humans too."

Mayes owns two dogs (dachshund-miniature pinscher twins Daisy and Dexter) and knows all his regulars by name. "There's Choncho, the peaceful French bulldog; Margarita, a rat terrier who I have become extremely close with; and 18 year-old Scrappy, whom I refer to as 'the shop elder.' He is so far the only one who knows his way straight to the treat box and never misses a chance to remind me."

Speaking of treats, no cosmopolitan canine who spends time looking over their owner's shoulder as they scroll through Instagram can have missed snaps of dog noses deep in Starbucks cups, eyes closed in bliss. The coffee superchain might have invented puppuccinos (an espresso cup of whipped cream), but Café/5 brought them to the artisan coffee shop world. This plant-filled neighborhood gem in Jefferson Park may not have a terrace, but it does offer delicious takeaway puppuccinos. Unlike the Starbucks ones, these are made with dairy-free cream and have a dog treat concealed in the middle—much better for dogs with digestion issues or diabetes. They're also served in a bowl for easier access.

CEO Shannon Kim has noticed that there are lots of bigger breeds in the area. She has a soft spot for a doberman named Apollo, who pops in every morning on his walk. "He's just the loveliest dog, we're really good pals with him. We have quite a few super-friendly dog/human regulars who really contribute to the atmosphere. My staff and I all love dogs and are always excited to meet them."

Another shop that belongs in your pooch's little black book is Stumptown Coffee Roasters. Go for a run around the Arts District Dog Park, which is privately managed and always immaculate, then head to Stumptown's shaded porch to enjoy one of its famous cold brews.

If your dog is going to take you out for coffee they want to know you're enjoying it as much as they are and with countless spots serving craft brews on shady terraces, it's a safe bet you'll find somewhere to keep you both happy. L.A.'s coffee scene is a dog's world—if you know where to look.

—

# The Sweet Life in Highland Park

WORDS
Julie Wolfson

PHOTOGRAPHS
David Maziarz

The history of coffee culture in Highland Park, now home to one of the most diverse coffee bar scenes, is steeped in the bakeries and coffee bars that have served the community for generations.

Highland Park was annexed to Los Angeles in 1895 to create one of the city's first suburbs. Nestled below the San Gabriel Mountains along the Arroyo Seco, a 25-mile-long riverbed canyon and watershed, Highland Park became home to Angelenos that wanted to move away from the city center. In the 1940s a shift in zoning laws led to many homes being replaced with multi-family dwellings. The arrival of the Arroyo Seco Parkway, the first freeway in the United States, contributed to a demographic shift. Many Mexican-American families eager to leave the dense city center relocated to Highland Park, north of downtown near Pasadena. Homes, apartments, and bungalow courts sprouted up as well as churches, restaurants, and cafes. Since the 1970s the neighborhood has been a hub for Chicano artists, including painter Carlos Almaraz and printmaker Richard Duardo. Later, in the 1980s many immigrants arrived from Guatemala, El Salvador, Honduras, and Nicaragua. As each generation moved to Highland Park, they opened businesses that served sweet pastries, like *pan dulce,* and coffee.

Javier Cabral, the editor of the award-winning local news and culture publication L.A. TACO, lives in Highland Park with his wife Paola Briseño-González. When asked about the coffee drinking rituals in Highland Park, Cabral sees a connection to the neighborhood bakeries. "When talking about coffee in historically Latino neighborhoods, coffee culture is synonymous with *panadería* culture and with *pan dulce,*" says Cabral. "The *panaderías* in the neighborhood have always been the main hubs for the consumption of coffee. You buy your bag of *bolillos* for *tortas, conchas,* and a big Styrofoam cup of black coffee." In this tradition, Delicias Bakery & Some opened on Figueroa in 1990 and is still baking *pan dulce, tres leches* cake, *polvorones,* and *tortas* served with coffee from Patria Coffee Roasters and Buddha Beans Coffee Co.

A few times a day, Cabral walks along Figueroa Street from Avenue 50 to York with his beloved sheepdogs. "The coffee cup I see people holding the most is La Monarca coffee," says Cabral. "They sought out Oaxacan single-origin organic coffee to serve to people who might not normally drink that kind of specialty coffee. Their environment has always been very welcoming and inviting. I see neighbors, firemen, city workers, and sweet, older couples there. La Monarca does a good job of serving quality coffee at prices that appeal to Highland Park's old-school working-class communities." The first La Monarca opened in Huntington Park in 2006 and was the first *panadería* in Los Angeles to source high-quality Mexican coffees to serve with its award-winning baked goods. La Monarca now has a dozen locations around Los Angeles County.

Cabral occasionally visits the local coffee bars and bakeries near his house, from La Monarca and Civil Coffee on Figueroa to Tierra Mia on Monte Vista Street. "The turning point of Highland Park coffee culture here was definitely Café de Leche on York Boulevard," says Cabral. "Their name is in Español. They honored the neighborhood's Latino history."

Anya and Matt Shodorf, the owners of Café de Leche, have lived in Highland Park for more than 20 years and wanted to open an espresso bar close to home. As a child, Anya Shodorf remembers waking up to the smell of fresh *tortillas,* beans, and her mom

Kumquat Coffee

Panadería Delicia

*Left: Panadería Delicia, Right: Collage Coffee*

brewing coffee with a cloth strainer called a *colador de tela* at their home in Nicaragua. "My family on my mom's side is from Chontales, Nicaragua. Cattle country," says Anya Shodorf. "My uncles and grandparents raised show horses. They were farmers. My grandmother owned a bakery in town for years, so I grew up running around in her bakery as a child. During one of my mom's visits, I found out that they also grew coffee on their farm."

This surprised Shodorf—she didn't know about the family's coffee farm. "Out of the blue my grandmother started talking about all the different varieties of coffee. Her knowledge blew my mind," she adds. "I did not know she knew so much about coffee until she told me about her family growing coffee. She talked about Bourbon coffee with such sophistication, I was impressed. I said, *'Mami, se lo tenía bien guardadito.'* Mamá Rosa, as my husband calls her, just smiled with pride."

The Schodorfs opened Café de Leche on York Boulevard in Highland Park in 2008 before many of the other espresso bars. "We love great coffee and wanted to share our love of coffee with our community." In recent years, they have started roasting their own beans that they source from Ethiopia, Rwanda, El Salvador, Colombia, and Nicaragua. The cafe continues to be a neighborhood gathering place, while more shops and restaurants have opened nearby. Now Kumquat Coffee and Collage Coffee have joined them on York Boulevard.

Sweet options continued to join the Highland Park coffee landscape. In 2015 Ulysses Romero expanded his growing coffee company by opening a Tierra Mia Coffee on Monte Vista Street. Romero sources specialty coffee and roasts in house at his Lincoln Park headquarters. Tierra Mia's coffee menu features pour overs and cappuccinos as well as *horchata* lattes and frappes served with house-made muffins, croissants, and guava cheese pastries.

Also, in 2015 brothers Alex and Alan Morales were ready to find a permanent location for their growing coffee company that had been started as a series of pop-ups. The Morales brothers were born in Mexico and raised in Burbank. After working in specialty coffee, including as a part of the opening team for Handsome Coffee Roasters, they were ready to branch out on their own. They built a coffee cart and started doing events. While starting the search for a cafe space, they began looking in Highland Park. Alex went into the coffee shops and bakeries along Figueroa. "I learned that Antigua has been on Avenue 57th and Figueroa for more than 10 years," says Morales. "They specialize in Guatemalan-inspired foods, offering staples like *frijoles negros* and sweet *plátano frito* served alongside richly developed coffees exclusively from Guatemala."

"It's very common to see folks walk out with a light breakfast and a comforting *cafecito* with *crema y azúcar* in Highland Park," says Morales. "It's also important to note that many of the Mexican eateries in the area often had a *café de olla*-style drink (a spiced, coffee traditionally made in clay pots) available to pair with breakfasts and that Café de Leche on York Boulevard was one of the first to offer what's considered a third wave specialty coffee experience here."

Before opening, the Morales brothers walked along Figueroa and introduced themselves to the neighborhood to tell folks they were planning on opening a cafe. During their summer buildout in 2015, every Saturday morning they set up an espresso cart outside the storefront. They would buy dozens of *pan dulce* from Delicias Bakery & Some and give out free coffee and *conchas* to anyone who passed by. "This is how we met a ton of folks in the

*Café de Leche*

*Collage Coffee*

*Left: Alex & Alan Morales, Civil Coffee. Right: Savana Lee.*

neighborhood," says Morales. "In just a few weekends, we had a line before we even opened the gate for 'free coffee Saturday.' We made a few thousand espresso and milk drinks."

That summer was a memorable one for the Morales brothers. "We met the artists of the Future Gallery, who saved the landmark statue of Chicken Boy nearby on Figueroa. We made hot chocolate for tattoo artist Popeye the Inkman, who has a studio called Revival Tattoos across from Civil Coffee," says Morales. "We befriended Frank Baroni, born and raised in East L.A., he's the essence of cool with his perfectly slicked-back, jet-black hair, Americana ink all over, denim, and a white shirt with a wide collar, rolling up in a hot rod, then coolly sipping coffee. We met the *señoras* at the *panadería* who expressed a sense of pride for us. We met the CD1 reps, local artists, newly transplanted photographers, yogis, and families with their kids. We had the pleasure of connecting face to face and a handshake."

While all of this was happening in front, inside, they were transforming the light-filled space in this 1920s building into their ideal cafe. "The weekend we opened, we received the warmest welcome with a line out the door for most part of the day," remembers Morales. Their menu features coffee bar classics and specialty drinks that celebrate the neighborhood, like The Figueroa, made with espresso, sweetened condensed milk, and cinnamon. They serve this drink with a Maria cookie, a packaged grocery store cookie that is popular in Mexico and around the world. The food menu highlights include *chilaquiles*, t*acos de barbacoa*, and avocado toast on local Bubb & Grandma's bread. They source beans from their favorite roasters, including Coava, Heart, and Dune. A collaboration with Coava led to developing their own signature house blend. They also partnered with Coava to source single-origin coffees from Ethiopia, Honduras, Colombia, and Mexico, recently securing contracts of green coffee from Oaxaca and Chiapas.

Now near Civil on Figueroa, Kindness & Mischief Coffee, and Go Get Em Tiger have opened. "It's been exciting to see the area bubble up with various coffee concepts, each offering their own interpretation of a cafe experience," adds Morales. "Options for consumers are great and so is a little competition. I believe all boats rise, but each vessel navigates differently too." At Civil, the Morales brothers have looked out from behind their La Marzocco GB5 espresso machine to see people reading tarot cards at one table while a Bible study group meets at another. Local artists and creatives hang out, as well as neighborhood grandmas. "At Civil, we are creative, but we're not trendy," says Morales. "We embrace change, adapt, develop, and know evolution is a natural part of business and life, but there are principles that are timeless in hospitality and coffee. Understanding this while being authentic, vulnerable, and open has allowed us a special place in the heart of Highland Park. We will never be short of gratitude!" To foster goodwill in the neighborhood, Civil hosts a yearly anniversary *fiesta* with specialty drinks, culinary pop-ups, sweets, and presents for the community.

The thriving cafe culture in Highland Park spans generations, where *café* plus *concha* shared with neighbors, equals delicious.
—

# Crossing the Divide

WORDS
Chérmelle D. Edwards

PHOTOGRAPHS
Adam Goldberg, Daniela Velasco

Coffee and wine have quite a lot in common. Both are ancient drinks originating in specific regions. And with both, terroir plays a vital role in determining flavor and value. As a result, coffee and wine have accrued wide audiences. Yet, until recently, they've largely inhabited two different worlds in the beverage community.

But in the past half decade, they've started to merge.

Alan Gomez just wanted a place to hang out. His first idea was to build a bar that also served coffee. However, while waiting for a beer and wine license and the bar buildout, he opted to initially operate as a coffee bar named Commodity in the Zaferia neighborhood of Long Beach, California.

"Coffee spots generally cast a wider net and have a bigger audience than bars. So, to help build a following, I had 'coffee shop' in the bio, just to attract more people," says Gomez, who opened Commodity in the spring of 2017.

While it did attract more people, it also meant eventually diverting Gomez from his goal of having a cafe and bottle shop. But within a year of opening, he was serving beer and wine.

Becoming a business that served both coffee and alcohol wasn't particularly easy. He had to reshape the narrative of his space and manage the elitist image the wine industry struggles to escape. His efforts to create an approachable atmosphere began with the people behind the bar. Their knowledge makes Commodity not just a pretty place where people want to be seen, but a space that the people can come to learn and explore.

"The experience I want people to have at Commodity, novice or expert, is very easy going. We like to choose wines that taste great and are well priced; same goes for coffee," said Gomez.

Commodity Coffee

Commodity Coffee

Gomez admits acquiring a taste for coffee took some time, but once it took a hold of him he never let go. "I think a very high percentage of coffee drinkers and/or enthusiasts love drinking alcohol the same way they love drinking coffee. And for a lot of people, coffee is the gateway to refining your palate. I think people see coffee and want more of this heightened experience with a different beverage. The foundation is already there."

A few miles from Santa Monica Beach is the first location of Goodboybob Coffee Roasters. Surrounded by small businesses, it opened for day coffee drinkers who frequented the specialty coffee shop for morning starts and midday pick-ups. In November 2019, after three years, Goodboybob Coffee started to incorporate wine, extending its hours and providing guests a non-caffeinated option for an afternoon meeting or a drink after work.

Introducing a wine program to a coffee bar required customers to feel familiar with and trust the taste of the bar's team, said Ryan Fisher, Director of Operations. That includes picking coffees and wines with unique processes and great stories that inspire the team to talk passionately about them. The wine program primarily consists of organic and biodynamic wines from California winemakers with an emphasis on those from the Central Coast. These bottles are visibly featured at the flagship location and the recently opened Culver City location inside Citizen Public Market.

Wine director Natalie Friedman tries to make her tasting notes fun and approachable. For example, of an Alsatian wine with skin contact, she says, "I swear it tastes like Haribo peach rings, which mimics this insanely on-point bubblegum note of a Colombia Natural Green Tip Gesha [coffee] we served for a while. One aspect of the coffee program I wanted to mirror [in our wine program] is attention to the narrative of each coffee farm and varietal. [I keep that] in mind when buying wine and talking about the process behind a bottle."

Goodboybob recognizes that coffee and wine aren't a new pair, but it is becoming increasingly common, especially in Los Angeles, where Fisher is excited to see wine become more accessible because of the context and space it can find with coffee.

As Goodboybob embraces both, Friedman observes that "the product is what brings people in, but the experience is what makes them come back. [Now], we're a coffee bar *with* wine, and in the evenings, a wine bar *with* coffee."

The corner bungalow on Painter and Mar Vista in Whittier, California used to be a deli before SALA converted the space into a public living room serving coffee and wine in June of 2019.

Owned by Brandee Raygoza and Derrick Montiel, SALA Coffee and Wine is within walking distance of two historic districts. The airy space is decorated with art from Cindy Suchite, but otherwise has a minimalist design.

There are chilled wines to the left and room temperature wines to the right. In the back is a paired down coffee bar with an espresso machine serving coffee from one of two roasting partners: Sey Coffee out of Brooklyn, New York and Little Wolf out of Ipswich, Massachusetts.

The decision to be a business serving both coffee and wine was born at home. "We've spent many days in our living room with folks who appreciate both beverages enough to have

Goodboybob

Brandee Raygoza, Sala Coffee and Wine

thought-provoking conversations about each one. It was a big life connector for us and continues to create community for us," said Montiel.

SALA opened not only to help its owners create a community, but to introduce it to those who might not have realized they needed one too.

"The majority of our customers were uninterested and maybe even intimidated by the idea. The more we started casually chatting about wine with our regulars (or anyone who seemed to show even the slightest interest in wine) the more the word seemed to get around," said Montiel. "Both coffee and wine attract a certain consumer, someone who goes out of their way to find a quality product. We felt like it was only a matter of time that everything would line up."

As they explored a deeper relationship with their coffee partner Sey, their sourcing methodology directly impacted how they wanted to approach the wines they bought. For example, they preferred buying a producer's entire vintage over specific bottles, and they focused on natural wine and transparency in sourcing.

On the cusp of an explosion of development in the West Adams district, Adams Coffee Shop opened in the fall of 2018 as a part of Alta, the restaurant by restaurateur Daniel Patterson and chef Keith Corbin serving California soul food. Adams Coffee Shop started as an all-day specialty coffee shop for the neighborhood carrying beans from Coffee Manufactory.

When Ruben Morancy moved from Northern California to become the wine director of Alta in the spring of 2020, he said that they "were trying to bend the business model [of the coffee shop] during the pandemic to a store, offering in-demand products." But, Morancy notes, "People weren't really coming here for that. We were known as a cafe."

Morancy then pitched the idea to Patterson and Corbin at Alta that they focus on selling wines made by women, like Faith Armstrong; women winery owners, women vine growers, and especially BIPOC winemakers, like The Brown Family Estate (the first African-American family who moved to Napa and purchased land), from Sonoma to Spain and as far as South Africa. While these wines make up 80 percent of their inventory, the remaining bottles come from male winemakers, as well as siblings and husband and wives duos.

"I'm not just buying wine because it's made by a woman. It has to be good; it has to be produced as naturally as possible—organic or biodynamic—and with minimal intervention. I like wines that are clean, not extremely funky but that are remnants of their true, varietal character, that have a sense of place and tell a story," said Morancy. Although coffee is still available here, in the middle of 2020, Alta fully embraced the wine-forward business by rebranding the coffee shop as Adams Wine Shop.

In Costa Mesa, Daydream Surf Shop is a multi-roaster and lifestyle shop offering coffee alongside surf culture.

Owners Kyle Kennelly and Rebecca Mantei wanted to answer the call from a community of customers asking for recommendations for a natural wine bar. So they opened Semi Tropic Wines in the spring of 2021, offering sun-washed vibes similar to those at Daydream.

Like the coffee that Daydream sources, which has a strong sense of place, the terroir of the wines selected by wine director Stephen Amato Salvatierra focuses strictly on organic and biodynamically farmed grapes from winemakers who embrace progressive standards and thoughtful processing.

"There's a lot of overlap between coffee and wine. Specialty coffee isn't just focused on exceptional quality at every step, from farming to dialing in espresso, it's also focused on ecological stewardship and creating an industry that's more sustainable for those growing coffee," said Kennelly.

Looking back to his high school days of drinking wine with his family, he recounts that he hadn't yet experienced the possibilities of what wine could taste like. That changed years later when he was introduced to natural wine along with the ethical components of winemaking, including the impact of low-intervention vinification. It's as if that gentle nudge into the spectrum of wine went on a first date with his reverence for coffee. And he fell in love.

These days, the pursuit of nuance in specialty drinks drives consumers to seek out establishments that can provide unique and diverse experiences. "If you appreciate good beverages you're going to be looking for shops that have progressive coffee programs, breweries that are pushing the envelope on quality, bars that have creative cocktails, and wine bars that are turning you on to cool stuff too. It's all connected and it's moving towards a more conscious consumption of everything. We want to stoke out the Napa cab dads enjoying a glass after golf as well as the skater kids in their twenties passing around a *porrón* at a house party."

The audience for both coffee and wine isn't on the horizon, it has arrived. There is a tangible movement in which the narrative of both is being reframed to include each other. Sommeliers are eagerly seeking out coffee shops as new outlets for wine and kinship with baristas, who are rapidly becoming L.A.'s new generation of owners and operators. And in so doing, coffee shops are reaching a broader audience.

—

# Riding Coffee's Sixth Wave on the California Coast

WORDS & PHOTOGRAPHS
Lucas Oliver Oswald

Malibu isn't all surf wagons and beachfront property. Tucked out of view from the coast is a wild side, a dry and dusty corner of Los Angeles, at times a landscape of green chaparral and manzanita. For now, and for the foreseeable future, the Santa Monica Mountains are burn-country, all rock and bare dirt, sparse and charred from wildfire that is increasingly becoming a part of life in Los Angeles.

Strange things can be found up here. Long the refuge of Los Angeles's more eccentric millionaires, bizarre estates sit atop mountain peaks and old film sets linger out of sight. Amongst these oddities is also a biological phenomenon—a coffee farm budding in a far corner of Malibu's mountains.

Coffee is a tropical plant that grows in equatorial regions of heavy seasonal rainfall and dense humidity. Until recently, it had never been cultivated in the continental United States. And yet, coffee grows here in Los Angeles.

Hidden away in the Santa Monica Mountains is Xanabu, the passion project of architect David Hertz and his wife Laura, a place that serves as a home, farm, camp-site, and now coffee plantation.

Xanabu is the stuff of Malibu lore. Visiting the property feels like paying tribute to California royalty—May Rindge, who once owned most of Malibu, won the right to build a hunting lodge there, in which David and Laura now live. The opposing hillside is home to a collection of makeshift pagodas, East Asian antiques, and set pieces from "The King and I," all comprising a dream-like village of confused oriental paraphernalia by the ranch's previous owner, famed artist and set designer Tony Duquette.

On another hillside is a large rectangle of green, an anomaly on the desert landscape. This is a crop of coffee plants, interspersed with various other foliage, each pea plant, shrub, and grass stalk serving a different, restorative purpose.

Hertz and his resident green-thumb Jorge Real Garcia showed me around the field, home to 550 coffee plants. Garcia looked like a modern-day cowboy, squinting at the horizon, the gnarled rock faces of the Boney Ridge framed behind him, and Hertz like a wizened surfer, long greying hair tumbling in the wind, hands brushing past the foliage at work below.

Nine months ago the coffee plants were doing well, each of them knee to waist high, thriving in Malibu's generous sunshine. The Woolsey Fire may have spared Xanabu, but the wind that spurred it did not. Eighty-five mph winds beat down the crop, stripping the plants of their foliage. Today, most of them are bare, not dead, but far from lush.

Garcia, originally from Mexico, has worked this land since before Hertz bought it. Coffee was no stranger to him—his father had a coffee farm in Jalisco.

"You could throw a coffee bean on the ground and it would grow," he said of his father's fertile land. The ground here in Malibu, on the other hand, was inhospitable and mostly rock, he explained. He looked pityingly over the struggling plants before us.

"We had to use a jackhammer to open it up."

Elsewhere on the Southern California coast, coffee agriculture is thriving. An hour north of Malibu in Santa Barbara, another haven for wealthy Angelenos seeking reprieve from the concrete jungle, coffee is creeping up in small crops on the edges of avocado orchards and pulling in a steep premium.

Jay Ruskey, Frinj Coffee

This is entirely thanks to Jay Ruskey. Born and raised in Los Angeles, Ruskey started working with avocados when he was 18 and quickly moved on to cherimoyas, a green heart-shaped fruit native to South America that is now commonplace at local farmers markets.

Ruskey had a large part to play in popularizing California cultivation of the cherimoya, as well as the passion fruit, dragonfruit, and now caviar lime, a finger shaped citrus that contains small, caviar-like beads.

For the past 20 years Ruskey has been taking on coffee, perfecting not just his cultivation methods but also his processing technique. It wasn't until recently that a market opportunity actually developed for California coffee. Though his coffee plants were still fickle, Ruskey found that the coffee did well when interplanted among his avocado farm.

"If you can grow avocados in California," he said, "it tells me there is a good chance you can grow coffee on your land."

In 2017, Ruskey incorporated Frinj Coffee and began recruiting avocado farmers to grow coffee. He had a good proposition—his coffee was fetching astronomical prices for its quality and unique story. With Ruskey supplying the plants and expertise, other farmers could grow coffee on their land, adding a big supplemental boost to their farm income with the specialty coffee.

Today, Frinj works with more than 70 farms between Santa Barbara and San Diego.

In the early days of specialty coffee, those in the know used to talk about the industry in waves. The first was defined by Folgers and Maxwell, home-brew that said nothing of tasting notes or origin. Starbucks stirred up the second wave, emphasizing quality and some degree of production location. The third wave included today's well-known specialty roasters, the Blue Bottles and the Stumptowns. Some say that the fourth wave is characterized by coffee brewing science and advanced equipment, while the fifth wave refers to the large-scale, commercial scaling of boutique coffee, like Blue Bottle's acquisition by Nestlé and the rapid expansion of its retail storefronts.

"I don't believe in waves," Ruskey told me. We were touring one of Frinj's network farms on the outskirts of Santa Barbara. "I'm a surfer. I believe in swells and microwaves. But if there was a fifth wave of coffee, COVID killed it."

Ruskey reluctantly defined Frinj as the beginning of a sixth wave. The same way California grape farmers were once called crazy for trying to replicate French wines, Ruskey sees a future in which California farmers disrupt the coffee industry with hyper-specialized and hyper-local coffee production. Coffee farm experiences, tours, and tasting rooms could provide a similar experience to modern wineries, justifying the absurd price of a California grown cup of coffee.

Grown in regions of cheap land and labor in the global south, coffee has always been an inexpensive commodity. At the time of writing, a pound of green coffee on the commodity market costs about $1.43 per pound. So what happens when you grow coffee in the Golden State, known for its skyrocketing real estate prices? Look no further than Frinj coffee, where green coffee regularly goes for over $75 per pound and up to $450, and a five-ounce bag of roasted coffee costs between $50-$80.

But after an afternoon spent at Good Land Organics, Ruskey's long-time farm and home to Frinj's processing facility for coffee harvested at all of the 70+ network farms, I'm beginning to think that price is justified.

Cascading down a hillside on the outskirts of Santa Barbara, Good Land Organics is a testament to the agricultural abundance of California. Coffee, passion fruit, avocado, cherimoya, dragon fruit, caviar lime, are all planted together in a sunny jungle of fruit. One thriving coffee tree would have been impressive, but there were hundreds, each one a different rare varietal bursting with red, ripened fruit.

As we made our way down the hillside, Ruskey handed me ripe coffee berries, explaining the differences between varietal beans. When ripe, coffee berries are sweet and delicious, and Ruskey's rare varietal beans each have a distinct flavor, some of them peppery and others rich like a ripe peach.

Ruskey may look like a farmer, but his approach is scientific, a modality that stretches into the complex processing coffee undergoes after harvest. Traditionally, coffee processing takes place across the supply chain by many different players, offering myriad opportunities for neglect, shortcuts, and ignorance to take their toll on quality.

Take storage for example. After it's processed, a green coffee bean sits in onsite storage subject to heat and humidity, followed by exportation, sitting in burlap sacks on a freighter ship sometimes for months. Finally it reaches the importer's storage facility and then the roaster where it will continue to rest, largely unmonitored, until roasted.

At Good Land Organics, the coffee is grown walking distance from where it is processed and roasted. The optimal amount of storage and aging time for the green bean has been tested and perfected, taking place in a controlled environment with a carefully selected temperature, humidity level, and air flow. This is true for the entire process. Unprecedented levels of care are taken at each step. Beans are sorted not once, but three times. The pH balance of the fermentation process has been measured and standardized. If there is a step to scrutinize, Ruskey has done it.

The result is what might be the perfect cup of coffee, if not for the price.

Inside his tasting room, Ruskey painstakingly prepared me a pour over. The coffee was divine—sweet, layered, and nuanced. I could easily imagine a sommelier serving it with flowery explanation.

Behind the bar I spotted a sign with the price per cup for visitors: $16. Still, $16 is a bargain compared to the $35 cups of Frinj coffee grown by singer-songwriter Jason Mraz on his Southern California ranch and sold at Bird Rock Coffee Roasters in San Diego.

And yet, there is a market for Frinj, and the California farmers cultivating it are reaping the benefits. So far Frinj farmers yield up to twelve times more profit per acre than their avocados, an unheard of return for farmers. This is a big part of Ruskey's motivation. He is committed to all farmers in his network receiving at least 50% of the profit from the beans he sells, an unprecedented percentage for an industry that regularly sees farmers fetching fractions of a cent on the final price of their coffee. For now, this means a fully vertical, direct-to-consumer company model. Aside from Mraz's coffee sold at Bird Rock, Frinj is entirely sold online.

David Hertz & Jorge Real Garcia, Xanabu

According to Ruskey, there is more than enough demand for California grown coffee to meet supply, even at the unusually high price it commands. With more coffee farms constantly being added though, it's unclear when supply will exceed demand, but Ruskey is confident that point is still far off.

In Malibu, walking among the coffee field at Xanabu, David Hertz referenced the wild profits he stood to make with the crop.

"Even with just one acre," he said, "with half the market rate and half the productivity rate, it's still potentially a $800,000 per year crop, which you can't even get with cannabis."

Hertz would like to see a return on his investment, but the primary driver behind his endeavor is far from profit.

For Hertz, the changing climate is top of mind. Unpredictable heatwaves, drought, wildfire, and strong winds are increasingly the new normal, but with Hertz's experience in sustainable architecture and restorative landscaping, he knows the potential benefits of well-cultivated land.

Coffee is far from the only change he's making, but he believes it might be the key. Hertz imagines an edible food forest like the one at Good Land Organics, the entire ecosystem at Xanabu transformed by restorative agriculture.

The potential of all this work is already clear. The earth is already rich, dark, and fertile. Surrounding the coffee are fences draped with thriving passion fruit vines providing shelter from the wind, and all around us are newly planted pepper, madrone, oak, and olive trees, creating a cool, humid microclimate. In Hertz's eyes, coffee has the potential to transform Xanabu into an oasis, protected from wildfire and other extreme weather events.

Hertz estimates he's spent around $150,000 just getting the coffee field started. Despite the work and the cost, he's undeterred. Like Ruskey, he seems only spurred on by the challenge.

Sitting with Hertz beneath Xanabu's otherworldly pagodas, I asked if he thought others in Malibu might take up coffee farming one day.

"Yeah, I think so," he said, "If we can prove it."

Like Ruskey, Hertz imagines a full-fledged coffee experience at Xanabu. Visitors would tour the farm and enjoy a cup of Malibu coffee in the shade of the pagodas. Xanabu would be fully transformed into a fertile, edible forest. A coffee plant might take no work at all to establish—just as Garcia said of his father's coffee farm in Jalisco, all Hertz would have to do is drop a coffee bean on the ground and nature would do the rest.

That future is far off, but Hertz is well on his way. I asked him if the young plants had yielded enough beans yet to squeeze one cup of coffee out of the crop.

He laughed.

"No, not yet," he said. "It'll be the most expensive cup of coffee anyone's ever had though."
—

# Keeping Waves at Bay

WORDS
Austin Langlois

PHOTOGRAPHS
Adam Goldberg, Daniela Velasco

For anyone looking at the map, Long Beach looks like it's just part of the urban sprawl of Los Angeles. As its name implies, it's a beach town that's sandwiched between Orange County and Los Angeles, sheltered by the world's longest breakwater, which keeps the waves at bay—literally. The calm harbor is home to the largest and second-busiest shipping port in the U.S., which supports the city's larger industries like aerospace and oil. And you don't have to look far to see the city's industrial side: take for instance the four islands off the coast, decorated with sculptures, palm trees, tall towers and colorful lights at night. They're not resorts, they're oil islands, which conceal the 24/7 active oil drilling and pumping.

The city also holds the rank as the seventh most-populous city in California, and is also a cultural hotspot, with deep roots in LGBTQ+ history, the largest Cambodian population outside of Cambodia, the only museum in the country dedicated to contemporary and modern Latin American and Latino art (MOLAA), and an eclectic array of historical and artsy neighborhoods. Here, it's easy to forget you're only 20 miles away from the City of Angels.

"Long Beach is its own scene," says Juliette Simpkins of Black Ring Coffee Roasters. "We don't have outwardly expanding hip neighborhoods like Silverlake and Highland Park. We have a melting pot of cultures. We became a brewery hotspot in the last five years. We have great Filipino soul food, chef-driven cuisine, and an ever expanding list of the 'next thing' pop ups."

\*\*\*

Like many suburban cities within a larger metro area, Long Beach has experienced a boom in development in recent years—

Rose Park Roasters

Black Ring Roasters

and with that comes the challenge of maintaining the "small-town charm" that its residents are so proud of.

The friendly, local-first atmosphere is evident in the city's craft coffee scene. Even as new competitors pop up, roasters are still quick to give a shout out to their coffee peers in the community, an attitude of independence—yet friendly collaboration—that feels more akin to the indie music scene than the restaurant business.

"The coffee scene here is very much in line with the style of the city—it's local and it's friendly," describes Wade Windsor, of Lord Windsor Coffee.

Today, coffee lovers might know Lord Windsor Coffee from its vibrant, tropic-forward coffee bean (and canned cold coffee) packaging. But when it first opened, Windsor's roastery and cafe, about a 10-minute walk from Alamitos Beach, was a bit of an anomaly among all the Starbucks in the area.

"We've been open since 2012, and at that time there was nothing in the way of craft coffee," Windsor continues. "I'm not making any formal claims, but it seems like once we opened our doors it let the floodgate open to new shops in new neighborhoods."

Windsor is also quick to give props to other roasters in town. "I consider the guys at Rose Park Roasters to be close friends, and strongly respect and admire what they're doing," he says. "They take the coffee so seriously and it shows. I also think Recreational Coffee is badass; their take on wonderful coffee gives room for more fun applications and styles of drinks. Steelhead Coffee and Commodity are also class acts; their take on a multi-roaster format gives new breath to the scene here and it's lovely."

Rose Park Roasters, the other pioneer to the Long Beach craft coffee scene, first started as a bean-by-bike delivery service. Andrew Philips then opened its first location on Fourth Street, nestled among Craftsman style bungalows. And with the neighborhood's highly walkable-bikeable reputation, they've continued to deliver coffee by bike across Long Beach (for free)—even during the COVID-19 pandemic.

It's people like Windsor and Philips who have paved the way for new roasters and specialty cafes in the city. Trevor Moisen, Simpkin's business partner at Black Ring Coffee Roasters, is quick to credit both as inspiration for their own roastery. "We literally wouldn't exist without these guys," he says.

Moisen and Simpkin opened up Black Ring in North Long Beach, an area they described as "underserved." Since their opening, the community connection has become a big part of Black Ring Coffee Roasters's identity. Before the pandemic, the cafe was a common meeting place for all sorts of folks. It's known by locals for latte art throwdowns and brewing coffee classes. A local council member even held a community meeting at the cafe. "We've never made real money with Black Ring, but we're doing what we love and have created an ethos and community we're intensely proud of," said Simpkin.

\*\*\*

You might think that the recent expansion within Long Beach over the past decade would affect the vibe of the community. And it still might. But for now, Simpkins, Windsor, and Moisen still see the Long Beach of yesteryear sticking around for years to come. In fact, Windsor seems to think that the increasing buildout of the city could actually be a net positive for the community.

"Long Beach is the least 'beach' town of beach towns with an attitude like nowhere else," said Wade Windsor, of Lord Windsor Coffee. "It's changing quickly with a lot of development and money pouring in. But, it feels like that undercurrent of change is solidifying locals to support and cherish their independent businesses that make up this city."
—

*Los Angeles:*

6IXTHSENSE
3881 W 6th St,
Los Angeles, CA 90020

Adams Wine & Coffee Shop
5357 W Adams Blvd,
Los Angeles, CA 90016

Alfred Coffee
8428 Melrose Pl,
Los Angeles, CA 90069

Amara Kitchen
519 N Avenue 64,
Los Angeles, CA 90042

Antigua Bread
5703 N Figueroa St,
Los Angeles, CA 90042

Bar Nine
3515 Helms Ave,
Culver City, CA 90232

Black Ring Coffee Roasters
5373 Long Beach Blvd,
Long Beach, CA 90805

Blackwood Coffee Bar
7509 Sunset Blvd,
Los Angeles, CA 90046

Blue Butterfly Coffee Co.
351 Main St,
El Segundo, CA 90245

Blue Bottle
1103 Abbot Kinney Blvd,
Venice, CA 90291

Bloom & Plume Coffee
1638 W Temple St,
Los Angeles, CA 90026

Café/5
2025 West Jefferson Boulevard
Los Angeles, CA 90018

Café de Leche
5000 York Blvd,
Los Angeles, CA 90042

Café Dulce
134 Japanese Village Plaza Mall,
Los Angeles, CA 90012

Canyon Coffee
Online-based roastery
Los Angeles, CA

Cindy's Eagle Rock
1500 Colorado Blvd,
Los Angeles, CA 90041

Civil Coffee
5629 N Figueroa St,
Los Angeles, CA 90042

Cognoscenti Coffee
6114 Washington Blvd,
Culver City, CA 90232

Collage Coffee
5106 York Blvd,
Los Angeles, CA 90042

Commodity
1322 Coronado Ave,
Long Beach, CA 90804

Compelling Coffee
1737 N Las Palmas Ave #100,
Los Angeles, CA 90028

Daydream
1588 Monrovia Ave,
Newport Beach, CA 92663

Dayglow
866 Huntley Dr,
West Hollywood, CA 90069

Delicias Bakery and Some
5567 N Figueroa St,
Highland Park, CA 90042

Destroyer
3578 Hayden Ave,
Culver City, CA 90232

Dinosaur Coffee
4334 Sunset Blvd,
Los Angeles, CA 90026

Doubting Thomas
2510 W Temple St,
Los Angeles, CA 90026

Eggslut
317 S Broadway,
Los Angeles, CA 90013

Endorffeine
727 N Broadway #127,
Los Angeles, CA 90012

Frinj Coffee
1362 Farren Rd,
Goleta, CA 93117

G&B Coffee
317 S Broadway C19,
Los Angeles, CA 90013

Gjusta
320 Sunset Ave,
Venice, CA 90291

Goodboybob Coffee
2058 Broadway,
Santa Monica, CA 90404

Goodboybob Coffee
9355 Culver Blvd,
Culver City, CA 90232

Go Get Em Tiger
5916 N Figueroa St,
Highland Park, CA 90042

Hi-Fi Espresso
227 CA-1,
Hermosa Beach, CA 90254

Highly Likely
4310 W Jefferson Blvd,
Los Angeles, CA 90016

Honey Hi
1620 Sunset Blvd,
Los Angeles, CA 90026

Hot & Cool Cafe
4331 Degnan Blvd,
Los Angeles, CA 90008

Intelligentsia
1331 Abbot Kinney Blvd,
Venice, CA 90291

Jones Coffee Roasters
693 S Raymond Ave,
Pasadena, CA 91105

Klatch Coffee
306 S Pacific Coast Hwy,
Redondo Beach, CA 90277

Kindness & Mischief Coffee
5537 N Figueroa St,
Los Angeles, CA 90042

Kumquat Coffee
4936 York Blvd,
Los Angeles, CA 90042

LAMILL
1636 Silver Lake Blvd,
Los Angeles, CA 90026

La Monarca
5833 N Figueroa St,
Los Angeles, CA 90042

Lavender & Honey Espresso Bar
1383 E Washington Blvd,
Pasadena, CA 91104

Lord Windsor Coffee
1101 E 3rd St,
Long Beach, CA 90802

Maru Coffee
1936 Hillhurst Ave,
Los Angeles, CA 90027

Maru Coffee
1019 S Santa Fe Ave,
Los Angeles, CA 90021

Mel's Coffee Shop
1660 N Highland Ave,
Los Angeles, CA 90028

Menotti's Coffee Stop
56 Windward Ave,
Venice, CA 90291

Moon Juice
2839 Sunset Blvd,
Los Angeles, CA 90026

Muddy Paw
3320 Sunset Blvd,
Los Angeles, CA 90026

Neighborhood
133 South La Brea Ave,
Los Angeles, CA 90036

Original Pantry Cafe
877 S Figueroa St,
Los Angeles, CA 90017

Patria Coffee Roasters
108 Alameda St,
Compton, CA 90221

Peach Pit
7507 Melrose Ave,
Los Angeles, CA 90046

Phoenix Bakery
969 N Broadway,
Los Angeles, CA 90012

Romancing The Bean
3413 W Magnolia Blvd,
Burbank, CA 91505

Rose Park Roasters
3044 E 4th St,
Long Beach, CA 90814

Rubies+Diamonds
6115 Sunset Blvd #150,
Los Angeles, CA 90028

SALA Coffee and Wine
3853 Atlantic Ave,
Long Beach, CA 90807

Saugus Cafe
25861 Railroad Ave,
Santa Clarita, CA 91355

Scoops Ice Cream
727 N Broadway Adult Stacks,
Los Angeles, CA 90012

Semi Tropic Wines
816 W19th Street,
Costa Mesa, CA 92627

Sesame L.A.
936 N Hill St,
Los Angeles, CA 90012

Seven Syllables Coffee
Online-based roastery
Cerritos, CA

Silverback Coffee of Rwanda
1712 Sunset Blvd,
Los Angeles, CA 90026

Sip & Sonder
108 S Market St,
Inglewood, CA 90301

Smoky Hollow Roasters
118 Sierra St unit c,
El Segundo, CA 90245

Sqirl
720 N Virgil Ave #4,
Los Angeles, CA 90029

Stumptown Coffee Roasters
806 S Santa Fe Ave,
Los Angeles, CA 90021

Superba Food and Bread
1900 Lincoln Blvd,
Venice, CA 90291

Ten
4065 Glencoe Ave #100,
Marina Del Rey, CA 90292

Thank You Coffee
938 N Hill St,
Los Angeles, CA 90012

The Assembly Cafe
634 N Robertson Blvd,
West Hollywood, CA 90069

The Boy & The Bear Coffee Roastery
350 N Pacific Coast Hwy,
Redondo Beach, CA 90277

The Palm Coffee Bar
2922 W Magnolia Blvd,
Burbank, CA 91505

The Reverse Orangutan
440 E Rte 66,
Glendora, CA 91740

The Rose
220 Rose Ave,
Venice, CA 90291

Tierra Mia
5528 Monte Vista St,
Los Angeles, CA 90042

Two Guns Espresso
3516 Highland Ave,
Manhattan Beach, CA 90266

Verve "Roastery Del Sur"
500 Mateo St #102,
Los Angeles, CA 90013

Woodcat Coffee Bar
1532 Sunset Blvd,
Los Angeles, CA 90026

Xanabu
28128 Pacific Coast Hwy #9,
Malibu, CA 90265

Yes Plz
3821 S Santa Fe Avenue
Vernon, CA 90058

**

*This list represents coffee shops visited, referenced, or interviewed on background for the making of Drift, Volume 11: Los Angeles*

*Outside Los Angeles:*

B&W
314 Brooks St,
Wake Forest, NC 27587

Bird Rock Coffee Roasters
5627 La Jolla Blvd,
La Jolla, CA 92037

Calendar Coffee Roasters
Unit 1, Ahaglugger, Barna, Co.
Galway, H91 X6CD, Ireland

Coava
1300 SE Grand Ave a,
Portland, OR 97214

Coffee Collective
Kristen Bernikows Gade 2, 1105
København, Denmark

Devoción
69 Grand St,
Brooklyn, NY 11249

Dripp
500 N Harbor Blvd Suite B,
Fullerton, CA 92832

Drop
Wollmar Yxkullsgatan 10, 118 50
Stockholm, Sweden

Dune
528 Anacapa Street,
Santa Barbara, CA 93101

Espresso Republic Coffee Roastery
4300 Edison Ave,
Chino, CA 91710

Heart
923 SE Hawthorne Blvd,
Portland, OR 97214

House Roots Coffee
16155 San Fernando Mission Blvd #3832,
Granada Hills, CA 91344

Little Wolf
125a High St,
Ipswich, MA 01938

Manhattan
Industrieweg 71, 3044 AS
Rotterdam, Netherlands

Port City Coffee Roasters
801 Islington St,
Portsmouth, NH 03801

Prolog
Høkerboderne 16, 1712
København, Denmark

Sey
18 Grattan St,
Brooklyn, NY 11206

Sightglass Coffee
270 7th St,
San Francisco, CA 94103

Tandem Coffee & Bakery
742 Congress St,
Portland, ME 04102

**

*This list represents coffee shops visited,*
*referenced, or interviewed on background*
*for the making of Drift, Volume 11:*
*Los Angeles.*

INSTAGRAM
@driftmag

TWITTER
@driftny

FACEBOOK
/driftny

WEBSITE
www.driftmag.com